"Loon Moments"
Broadcasts on Life
Copyright © 2009 Scott Franz

SnoppyQwop Press
PO Box 1429
West Point, VA 23181

Paperback ISBN: 978-0-578-01246-9

Printed in the United States of America

Lulu ID #6102538

Direct Inquiries to: www.authorscottfranz.com

["LOON MOMENTS"]
Broadcasts on Life – by Scott Franz

To the Love of My Life,

Ann

Table of Contents

Forward I
December 2006

I first introduced the "Loon Moment" on my weekly radio show, "The Green Hour Show", which formerly aired every Saturday morning on News Talk 560 radio in Chicago.

When I broadcast the first "Loon Moment", I really didn't intend for it to be a weekly feature on the show. It was supposed to be a one-time airing. I had some "loon calls" recorded and sent over to the station and I wanted them to be played in the background as I told a story about a recent fishing trip up to the "Great North Woods". The response I received to the segment was phenomenal; calls, letters, e-mails from listeners, and the station's management, every bit of it positive. The "Loon Moment" was born that day and I swore to do a "Loon Moment" every week during the show for as long as I was on the air.

You'll hear me explain what the "Loon Moment" is about often as you read the many "Moments" in this book. Since many of them are the edited transcripts from live show segments, I often took the time to explain the "Loon Moment" for the benefit of new listeners. In some cases, I don't, so I'll take a moment now to explain.

I gave myself a lot of latitude in terms of what the "Loon Moment" could be about, but generally speaking it was about moments spent outdoors, either alone or with people I cared about. The settings occurred anywhere, from the most secluded wilderness to my own backyard. The activities that spawned any particular moment were varied as well, from a week of backpacking with family, to a sunset shared with my wife. But whatever the activity, or wherever the setting, in the end, a "Loon Moment" always, well mostly, brought me to some realization, something larger than the moment or the activity itself.

I'm a very conservative guy and WIND is a very conservative radio station, or at least it was in its infancy. So it shouldn't come as a surprise to any reader that many of the "Loon Moments" deal with a lot of similar and primarily conservative thoughts and themes. They dwell on the themes of God, family, country, friends, personal responsibility and character, all from my own conservative perspective. Some of them may seem a little preachy, but believe me, I'm not preaching, not by a long shot. Conservatives believe being judgmental is truly a necessary part of living. Not being personally perfect, or not always abiding by the standards you proclaim is no reason to discard those standards, throw out your ideals or stop making judgments about people's behavior. We have to be judgmental. To not be is well, liberal, and we've all seen how well liberal ideals work out and contribute to societal well being.

As you read these stories, you'll probably notice some pretty weird punctuation and grammar. When the "Loon Moment" aired on the radio there were pauses, exclamations and other types of verbal emphasis in the stories. I've tried to remove a lot of these during editing, but much of it remains as I tried to replicate the same emphasis in the printed word. The end result would make a bad

English teacher cringe and a good one cry. Some have been left just as they aired on the radio.

"Loon Moments" comes from the heart, my heart, and they poured out of me easily and effortlessly. I've spent a lot of time in the outdoors, both by myself and with friends and family. During those times, I've come to understand myself better, I've come to appreciate friends and family more, I've learned to appreciate the power and the beauty of nature, and most importantly, I've found God in all His glory. I hope you enjoy reading them as much as I've enjoyed writing them.

Scott Franz - December 2006

Forward II
Added February 2009

The original "Loon Moments", published in early 2007 was rushed to print. It was littered with a mass of editing errors and was cheaply and unprofessionally printed. To put it mildly, it was truly a writer's nightmare and I wasn't at all happy with the final product.

For starters, since a lot of the stories were actual transcripts of broadcasts I aired on the radio, there were the always present time constraints imposed on each story by the very medium of radio itself. While the station's management never once placed any limits on me or censored anything, there were some self- imposed constraints in addition to those imposed by time. There's just something about not knowing exactly who might be listening which seemed to temper my speech, not much, but a little. I can easily live with the knowledge I offend some people, especially liberals, but the possibility that children might be listening and perhaps misunderstand some of my rants and ravings, made me at least try to be somewhat cautious of the words and language I blasted out over the airwaves. I feel no such restraints in the written word. In any case, the sense of several "Moments" being incomplete or needing something more was overwhelming for me, and it nagged me from almost the very moment it first went to print. It finally nagged me into making this revision.

Procrastination rarely pays off for anyone, and in my case, up until now at least; I can say categorically, it's never paid off for me. But by a strange turn of chance, this time it did; at least from the point of view of a commentator. The current events of our day are truly momentous and transforming. The failure and collapse of our financial system and the resulting political events unfolding almost daily, threaten to obliterate the inspired vision our forefathers had for our country. Quite possibly, they threaten the very existence of our nation itself, at least as we've come to know it these past couple of centuries. If you think I'm exaggerating, I'd counter you're not paying attention, and don't recognize the truly earth shattering ramifications of these events for what they are. In any case, looking through the lens of today's events, it becomes even more important our country hold on very tightly to our basic principles, those which have made this country so very different from all the other nations of the earth.

In the end, if we're to save our country, I believe we'll need to resurrect and re-embrace those principles and values; the values dealing directly with God, Family and Country, those which bind us together as a people and provide us with a solid anchorage in this stormy, turbulent world. Many of the "Loon Moments" you'll read in this book speaks to those very principles; and I'm glad for the opportunity to re-emphasize their relevance in these troubling and tumultuous times.

Scott Franz – February 2009

One

"From Alter Boy to Atheist to God Again"

How does a pious little boy, raised to be devoutly Catholic both at home and in the Catholic schools, turn into a full-blown, church-dodging atheist by the time he reaches the age of sixteen, and while still attending a Catholic high school? Tell me if you can, how a former altar boy and former president of the St. Dominic De Salvo Fan Club (an obscure saint, I grant you), who like all good, young catholic boys of his day, had aspirations of joining the priesthood (Thank God that passed), comes to a point in life where he's absolutely certain that GOD doesn't exist. And not only is he dead certain of it, he knows something the poor, foolish, un-washed doesn't; God is merely a man-made idea; a stew-like concoction, a recipe made by mixing a pinch of dashed hopes, two cups of unfulfilled dreams, several gallons of human weakness, fill with desperation and season by adding the need of men and women with below average IQ's to believe in something beyond their own capabilities. It's a recipe mixed up in a big vat and stirred with a crutch. Of that he became certain.

Long before I ever read a book, *"The Case for a Creator"*, by Lee Stroebel, I had figured out the answers to those questions. I had long ago figured out that I had been the unwitting and unwilling subject of a very sophisticated brainwashing and surprisingly enough, a brainwashing aided by my Catholic educators.

The battle for the minds of our country's youth started long before I ever entered grammar school. The "Scopes Trial" was decided on July 21, 1925, years before my parents were even born. The "monkey trial" was a sensational and concocted show trial, but it served as the launching pad for Darwin's theory of evolution to be taught not only in our public schools, but in parochial schools as well.

In 1953, three years before I was born, Stanley L. Miller and Harold C. Urey, conducted what I like to refer to as "The Experiment". Their now discredited "Origin of Life" experiment created not only a whirlwind within the scientific community, but an air of almost dead certainty that science would soon completely solve all questions about the origins of life, and that God would most certainly be missing from those answers. The pictures of the learned man in a lab coat made their way into every primary education science book in the country, along with the fairy tale and insinuation of how they had been able to create the building blocks of life in a test tube. The timing and the publicity this experiment generated makes it, in my estimation, "The Experiment" of all time. This one experiment, and the resulting "Big Lie" it told then, and continues to tell to this day to successive generations of school boys and girls, particularly as it relates to the lies of Darwinism, has done more to create an army of atheists than any other scientific experiment conducted in the history of mankind. Still in school text books today, at least now one is able to find articles about the preposterousness of that experiment and the conclusions drawn from it.

In the late 1950's and early 60's, clergy and educators in religious schools didn't really stand a chance against the onslaught of the Darwinists. Although they tried their very best to keep my generation, the one coming of age in that time, grounded in religion and faith, they failed. They failed for a lot of reasons. I'll only give you two, but I'm sure you'll understand.

First, science and scientists were elevated to almost god-like status during that time and the technology boom we were experiencing only served to prove and add credibility to that status. The beginning of the space-age and the space race cemented their status as our young impressionable minds watched in awe and soaked up the images of those fantastic technological achievements. All scientific disciplines benefited from that age, as if somehow all scientific disciplines were all on equal footing. The prestige of scientists reached an all time high during this time, and of course, it would have been a form of heresy in itself to suggest that a scientist could, or would, ever lie. Certainly they would never fudge or fix the results of an experiment, or jump to any outrageous conclusions based on some personal or political agenda. So basically, this was the era science became "good", and science became "trusted", and science was "smart". Because science was good, trusted and smart, with only the noblest goals and the purest of motives, it started to be perceived by a whole generation as the only obvious path to ultimate truth.

Second, religious educators of my day either couldn't or didn't come up with very convincing ways to explain the contradictions we faced and the challenges to our faith, as we were presented with these new scientific "facts"; facts which ran into our traditional religious beliefs like two bull elk during mating season. While being told by our religious educators that our beliefs were not contradictory to science, science was telling us a completely different story. And the story was simply this: "God doesn't exist" and science provided or soon would provide the answers to all of mankind's questions. During this time, science definitely had the PR battle won. It was game, set and match. Remember, it was science that presented us with "facts". Science was good, it was trusted and it was smart. What kid wanted to be on the other side of an equation like that? The flip side of that coin was obviously bad, untrustworthy and stupid, and no one wanted to be painted with that brush. Yet if you even questioned the conclusions of the scientific community, which was now moving on a fast track towards atheism, there you were: an isolated, ignoramus who was not to be trusted. And that's exactly where religious educators and people of faith found themselves. They find themselves in the same place today, painted with the same brush.

And so it was with me. It was my pride, my "intellect", and my need to be considered "scientific" that took me away from God and the truth, and turned me into an atheist by the age of sixteen. I'm obviously using the term "intellect" loosely; as it was more a yearning to be viewed as an "intellectual" than it was anything close to true intellect. I certainly wasn't alone though in the way I thought and was maneuvered into atheism. I had a whole lot of company. An entire generation of my peers was under a constant barrage by educators and the media. New "discoveries" and new "facts" were constantly thrown at us. If we accepted them without question, each and every one of them reinforced and confirmed our status as "intellectuals". And why shouldn't we be receptive? It was all packaged and presented to us by the noble, unassailable group of wizards we came to know collectively as "science". Who could argue with "science"? Whose individual intellect or individual mental capacity could stand against or argue with the almost omniscient nature that pool of knowledge known as science represented? Sadly, not me; I wasn't smart enough to argue nor strong enough to withstand the heat.

So that's how I got conned by science, the press and educators and put God and my faith on a shelf for a lot of years.

Now, I liked Stroebel's book, "The Case for A Creator" a lot, and it makes some great intellectual arguments for believing in a God who created all things. It presents a new breed, if you will, of scientists, those with true intellect and an amazing grasp of a wide variety of scientific disciplines, who also demonstrate amazing critical thinking skills. They challenge today's scientists representing the status quo, whose views are being taught to our children, because they've come to the same conclusions about God I've managed to reach. I'm glad they're able to make the scientific arguments; I'm glad they're able to reach people with their intellect. But it was my "intellect" that got me off course in the first place and if people rely on intellect and intellect alone to know their Creator, they'll always be in danger of losing him again through the same "intellectual" process.

I myself came back to God in a much different way. I searched high and low for Him in every place I could imagine. I read and studied and experimented in a thousand different ways in my search for Him. I used every bit of my "intellect" to reason out His existence or lack thereof. And when I got done doing all those things, I still hadn't found Him. Finally, I was so tired and exhausted at trying to use my intellect and my reason.... I just did what I was told to do by God Himself. I looked at the lilies of the fields, I looked to the birds of the air and I looked to the things of nature. And there HE was in all His glory.

The following collection of "Loon Moments" represents thoughts of mine alone. Some of them you may have heard, as they're direct transcripts from various "Loon Moment" segments of my weekly radio show, "The Green Hour" on WIND in Chicago. Some have never been aired and some probably never will be. If I'm on the air long enough, perhaps you'll hear most all of them, but I doubt it, as new "Loon Moments" happen to me all the time.

Not all of the "Loon Moment" stories in this book are about my finding God in Nature, but some of them are. Some of them are just plain old stories that I decided to share with you. Take from them what you will; each one of them opened my eyes a bit in some way and I've tried to share those insights, however warped they may be, with you. Whatever you take from them, I hope you enjoy them in some way. They represent what's been a pretty interesting journey of discovery for me.

Scott Franz – July 2007 (Never Broadcast)

I wrote the above to broadcast, but I never got around to airing it. I wish I had. In retrospect, here's what I would have liked to have added:

This country is constantly being hoodwinked by BS science. I would offer as an additional example the entire "Global Warming" issue, but that's a whole new can of worms which I'm sure I'll get to later. I'll stick to the issue of the mangy, stinking, atheist, socialist, commie dogs ruining our country for now.

Ann Coulter's book "Godless" does a great job of exposing liberalism for what it truly is, a state sponsored pseudo-religion with all the trappings. So I'm not even going to get into the argument about liberalism being a religion-It is; and all of its bogus doctrine is continuously being shoved down the throats and into the minds of our children from preschool through college.

During the process of this religious indoctrination, our children are also continuously being brainwashed, under the guise of science, with the communist-socialist-atheist liberal agenda. High upon the dung heap of this agenda is the notion of "tolerance". The notion of "tolerance" or tolerating people who are different from you means that one has to be accepting of every demented, debased and perverted behavior known to mankind or risk being labeled "judgmental". I'm pretty sure in the church of liberalism; "judgmental" is the equivalent of a mortal sin to Catholics. The *reason we're required to be tolerant is that for each and every deviant behavior there's a good scientific reason for its existence, making the practitioner of it unable to control themselves, and thus, blameless. Science will someday find the "Homo Gene" that makes homosexual behavior unavoidable. Science will* <u>*always*</u> *find a mental disorder for whatever we seem to be unable to control. Eating, sleeping, drug and alcohol abuse, you name it, the good scientists of the church of liberalism will come up with some scientific dung to explain it.*

While I'm straying a little from the science theme here, let me remind you that the notion of "tolerance" is applied to all religious groups in the country as well, except to the vast majority of the inhabitants of this country, namely Christians. To get back on track, I'm sure someday they'll come up with a scientific reason why Christians should be persecuted; it's probably just waiting for some grant money funding as we speak. And while I'm on the topic, I've got some good scientific reasons of my own as to why the slimly, murderous, throat-cutting fascists in Islam should not be" tolerated". How about because they're trying to kill us at every opportunity, eh Dr. Obvious? I've got to tolerate a minaret going up in my neighborhood, a long standing symbol of Islamic conquest, under the guise of tolerance, while the entire Islamic world remains quiet about the evil doing of the terrorists. But God help me if my kid utters a silent prayer before he eats lunch in the school cafeteria. I've got to bail them out of jail and send them to diversity and tolerance training or they can't come back to school, and I've got to pay for it. One

Islamic taxicab driver complains and next thing you know we're installing foot washing stations in the airports on the taxpayers dime.

It's easy to get off topic and on a rant when discussing how the left is trying to turn this great country of ours into an immoral and godless nation with the willing cooperation of the atheist scientific community. Sir Isaac Newton and Einstein would be rolling in their graves if they could see what's happening in the name of science these days. They couldn't imagine separating God from science. Neither can I. I'm glad I found my way back to God and I pray that our country does as well. I hope Dennis Miller doesn't have this line copyrighted, but – that's just my opinion. I could be wrong.

Scott Franz – July 2007

Two
"Bear Cubs"

It is time once again for the "Loon Moment" segment of the show, and as you know by now, the "Loon Moment" is a time where we share with each other some of our experiences in the outdoors and nature. Mostly, I share with you, but the door is always open.

I've received an awful lot of feedback from listeners since I began doing the "Loon Moment", and most of it has been very positive; not all of it, but most of it. Oh, I get e-mails now and then from people who think I'm stupid and should be thrown off the air. It's been suggested that I try way too hard to be an intellectual, and that I'm far too big an ignoramus to pull it off. But, on balance, most of you seem to enjoy the "Loon Moment". All the same, I'm getting ready for the firestorm today.

Several years ago, I was canoeing and fishing in the boundary waters area along the US/Canadian border. I had entered from the Canadian side and had planned to canoe and fish for about a week, enjoying the solitude, eating fresh fish and soaking in a little nature. I had a loose plan to portage over to a different lake on one of my days "in country" to see some aboriginal drawings that were supposed to still be pretty visible. The plan was really loose because I wasn't really sure I wanted to drag a canoe over a mile and a quarter of rough, mosquito infested terrain just to see some smudged drawings of a pre-historic moose. But, after a few days of relaxing and fishing,

I decided it would be worth it to make the portage and see the moose smudges.

The following morning I rose early and ate a lumberjack breakfast of eggs, bacon, fresh bass and coffee. I didn't want to carry more than a snack as I would be struggling enough to haul the canoe and my other gear over the portage and I wanted to go a light as possible. Walking a mile and a quarter is nothing on flat ground, but dragging all of your gear and a canoe over rugged terrain that could only be called a trail if you used the term very loosely really takes a little doing, especially if you're alone. So anyway, well fed and with a blue sky overhead I set out to see the moose smudges.

The portage to "Moose Smudge Lake" was only a couple of miles away from where I was camped, and in the still, glass-like morning water, it took almost no time at all to reach the portage. I climbed out of my canoe and started to get psyched up for the portage.

I don't think anyone had been to see the moose drawings for some time, and certainly not during this season, because the portage was all overgrown with vegetation and blocked with fallen trees. I don't know how familiar you are with this part of the world, but I think it's probably best described as a "northern jungle", and going overland is no easy task. The bugs were out and beginning to bite and they were very much attracted to the sweat that was pouring out of me as I worked to drag my gear through the jungle.

I was getting a little irritated with myself for deciding to go through with all of this aggravation, but I soon came across a little clearing, the bugs seemed to go away and I stopped to rest for a moment. I noticed a patch of wild raspberries about ten yards away from me and I walked over to pick a few for a snack. Things were looking up and I figured the worse was over. That's when I noticed a steaming pile of bear dung near my feet.

I had only picked a few berries before I discovered the pile and I immediately froze, looked up from my berry picking, and saw the bear. She was a big cinnamon colored girl that looked to go about four hundred pounds. I could have been wrong about her weight, but when you're that close to a bear, they all look like they weigh four hundred pounds. Don't be impressed with the fact that I knew it was a female. I only found out right then because I saw her three cubs bouncing and bounding around in the berry patch only a few yards from me. That's when I really got nervous, and so did my cinnamon colored friend.

Now since I'm here to tell you this story, you can surmise that I survived this experience without any harm coming to either myself or the bear and I made it back to civilization. The mamma bear copped a major attitude though and I didn't get to see the moose smudges after all. The bear ended up going in that direction with her cubs in tow, and I ended up going back the way I came. It seemed to be a pretty good compromise and an acceptable deal at the time. I wasn't all that worked up to see the moose smudges anyway.

But the reason I thought of that mamma bear this week was because of some new news on the embryonic stem cell research front.

It appears that they can now extract stem cells from amniotic fluid without destroying the embryo itself. So if embryonic stems cells actually do hold out any promise for curing diseases in the future, it seems they can be obtained in a manner that should make everyone happy. Translation: There is no need to kill babies to harvest the stem cells that will likely create massive tumors anyway. We can create those massive tumors without killing babies. Or we can just use adult stem cells and cure a few diseases, your choice.

You may be wondering what in the world bears have to do with stem cell research? Not a thing. But I can absolutely assure you of this, and I was convinced of it beyond a shadow of a doubt, a 400 pound cinnamon colored bear was about to extract stem cells from me, all to protect her young, bouncing cubs. And I don't think the medical procedure she was about to employ was going to be so gentle or painless. I was about to have my stem cells harvested just because I happened to get within ten yards of her cubs.

In some ways, I think most people are a lot smarter than bears. We live in houses, drive cars, go out to dinner and have dental plans. Bears used to roam all over the North American continent; and now they're only in the wilderness areas. And they moved out because of us. Basically, we drove them out. If they were so much smarter than us, I guess we'd be living in the woods now and they'd have the air conditioning. But in other ways, I think bears may be a little smarter than people. If bears aren't any smarter, then maybe they're just a little nobler. They still try and protect their young.

I'll never understand the pro-abortion crowd. I just can't. No matter how hard I try to understand their point of view, it always falls short for me. I know all about the heart wrenching stories of unwanted pregnancies and I truly feel for the thousands of disadvantaged teenage mothers, but it can never justify infanticide for me. What other species kills their young for the sake of convenience? How did we come to accept the killing of our babies as normal, rational behavior?

There is nothing more un-natural than a mother killing her babies. Every time we see it in the news, we're horrified and astounded it could happen. And yet our society legally allows mothers to kill their babies in the womb. With all the post partum depression excuses flying around these days, we seem to want to extend the legality of a woman's "choice" to include kids up to six or seven years old. If this trend continues, I'm going to have to start looking over my shoulder when my mother comes over for dinner, and I'm over fifty. When will "choice" give way to some sanity? For those of us who weren't exactly mom's favorites, we'd like to feel safe again.

No, it's really not natural to kill your own children. Trust me. We're the only species on this planet that does it. Legal, yes. Natural, no. Natural is a fierce determination to protect your young at all costs. Natural is a display of violent rage at anyone who harms or even threatens to harm your children. If you don't believe me, you don't know a thing about nature and you've never come across a bear in a berry patch. And that is the "Loon Moment" for today.

From the "Loon Moment"- Broadcast in February 2007

Here's what I would have liked to have added:

"Woman's right to choose. Right! What a nice, clean, surgical term for a woman's right to sleep with men they wouldn't want to raise children with unless hell froze over. The right to then kill the product of that stupid choice, which by the way is undeniably a "human being" from the moment of conception until birth, because it would inconvenience them and keep them from going out to bars and finding more men to sleep with they would never want to have children with.

I love the argument from the pro-choice crowd that a newly created embryo isn't a human being. What the hell is it then? Do they really want to take the position that every time a woman gets pregnant it's some sort of wild "anything goes species lottery"? If it was, it would really bring new meaning to the term "expectant parents". What would they be expecting? "Oh honey, just think about it. If we're lucky we'll soon have a new....what - Labrador retriever?" If that we're the case, I think my wife and I wouldn't have stopped at four children. I know I would've wanted to keep trying for a Lab. They're great bird dogs and you don't have to support them with much of anything except a little dog food. With human children, you're stuck supporting them for a good 20-25 years. One thing's for sure, if the ultrasound ever showed that we were going to have kittens, I'd be all for abortion. I hate cats as much as I hate the pro abortion crowd.

Speaking of which, I absolutely despise the members of the "Pro-Choice Mafioso" and what they stand for, and I'm particularly offended by the grotesquely ugly female spokeswomen for abortion and the left in general. If anything could bring me around to being "Pro-Choice", it's the thought of them bringing even more grotesque people into existence by <u>NOT</u> allowing these women to have abortions. Not only are they physically repugnant, which makes me wonder why this is such a big issue for them anyway, I really doubt their dance cards are that full, but they constantly expose the inner ugliness of their souls every time they open their pie holes and yap at us about a woman's right to her own body.

By the way, did you know that NARAL used to be an acronym for "The National Abortion and Reproductive Rights Action League"? It's now "NARAL – Pro Choice America", where the NARAL apparently isn't an acronym for anything anymore. For all we know it could be a hair remover for women, "NARAL – smooth, silky legs, the choice of American women on the go". What the hell is that all about? I'll tell you what it's about; even though their own organization is about protecting abortion on demand, they can't even use the word "abortion" in their name because it's so damn offensive and they have to pretend like they're not "pro-abortion". Why is that anyway?

And why do politicians who run for national office have to dance around the abortion issue like ecstasy crazed teenagers in a mosh pit? It's a bitch trying to figure out a way to say you're not for abortion, but you are for a woman's right to have one whenever she wants, right up until the time of delivery. Why does the language of this debate have to be blanketed with nice sounding euphemisms? I'll tell you why, because we have to delude ourselves as people and as a nation as to what abortion really is and why we're allowing it to continue. It's that simple. We are absolutely appalled when we hear the Chinese people go out and drown their female infants. Who could possibly be so barbaric? I guess it's just better to delude oneself and call infanticide a women's health issue and something between a woman and her doctor.

I could go on forever about this issue, but I won't. On the radio, I told a story about a mamma bear and her cubs that I ran into in a berry batch up in the north woods. I was hoping it would make some people think about how unnatural abortion really is; how it defies our own human nature and God's divine laws to protect and nourish our young. I don't know if it did any good. Maybe I was being too cryptic and like the far left, not dealing with the issue head on. Some day this country will have to come to terms with this horrible evil. I hope it's soon.

Scott Franz – July 2007

Three
"Clues from our Creator"

Last weekend, I got a little musky fishing in up in the great woods of northern Wisconsin. Personally, I think us "musky fisherman" as a group, need to come up with another name for musky fishing, because between the four of us who went fishing, not one of us even saw a fish, much less caught one, not even one. I think it should probably be called something other than musky fishing, but that's not what the loon moment is about today, it just happens to be the setting for what inspired this weekend's "Loon Moment".

We were fishing one afternoon, and as afternoon turned into evening, there we were, still out on the lake. We continued fishing well into the evening. It had gotten pitch black out on the lake except for the crescent moon that was sending a very bright beam across the smooth surface of the lake, and I guess by that point we really weren't fishing all that hard, although we had some lines in the water, we were just kind of sitting in the boat, sipping on cold beer and watching the moon and the stars rise up into the early night sky.

There wasn't much talking going on between my fishing partner and myself, which is EXACTLY why I fish with him in the first place. We were just sitting there without speaking. As I stared up at the evening sky, more or less alone with my thoughts, I suppose he was relishing the time alone with his. Anyway, my thoughts were centered on a book I've been re-reading called "The Case for a

Creator" by Lee Stroebel. It's a book making the case for the intelligent design of the universe. By the way, if you've never read this book, you should. It's really very good, and for me, it was very descriptive about my own spiritual journey through life. But I digress. I was watching the moon and following the early evening stars rise out of the east; this right after witnessing probably the most magnificent, but brief sunset I'd ever seen. It almost looked as if there was a fire burning on the ground way out on the horizon. Anyway, it got me thinking about some of the things I had just re-read in Stroebels's book.

Now I really don't want to get into the intellectual arguments for intelligent design vs. evolution today, that's a very long and drawn out debate in and of itself and not really the point. I will tell you though, that as a scientific theory, "Darwinism" is probably THE most discredited theory ever put forth by ANY scientist at ANY time in the history of mankind; and why it is so desperately hung onto, and clung to by educators and scientists the way it is, well it's way beyond me. And by the way, I'll grant you that just because "Darwinism" is discredited; it by no means proves the case for "intelligent design". I doubt anyone could actually prove "intelligent design" if they wanted to, but for God's sake, the atheist scientific community should at least come up with another, and certainly a better theory on the origins of life, than stubbornly hanging onto Darwin's theory of evolution. It's just a rotten theory as science goes.

I do want to speak to what we, or at least the believers among us, intuitively KNOW if we really search our hearts, especially when we see some of the more awe inspiring things that nature has to offer. I mean, as I was watching the stars rise and the moon cast its light over those still, northern Wisconsin waters, there was absolutely no doubt in my mind whatsoever the universe was no accident, no freak of chance or some random occurrence. I knew it was created, and it was created for us to explore, and it was created for us to discover our Creator Himself. I've said often I think that we are meant to find God in nature – that we are supposed to look around both on this very, very, very unusual planet we've been given, AND that we are supposed to look out into the very cosmos themselves. The further we look and the harder we search, the more the evidence will reveal the Hand of our Creator.

By the way, some of the theories that have been put forth regarding the possibility of life on other planets have really started to be somewhat discredited themselves, and the uniqueness of our little "blue planet" and its ability to sustain life - human, plant and animal life is not something that seems very likely throughout the rest of the universe. The universe is a harsh, violent place and science is getting confirmation almost daily on just how unique a place our little earth really is.

I personally find it so very funny that the wacko environmentalists seem to worship the very earth itself while completely ignoring the Creator who made it. Think how primitive and aboriginal the concept really is. THINK, in this day and age, of actually worshiping a River god, or a Sun god or a Moon god or the god of the Volcano, or WHATEVER. Think of the limited intellect and lack of understanding it takes to worship objects like that, and yet that's exactly the mindset of the left and their religion of environmentalism. They ridicule those who would look for and can actually see their Creator and His hand, behind all the marvels of nature, as being dolts and ignoramuses and as lacking in intellect.

But we really know it's those with limited intellect and an inability to think in the abstract that can't see the hand of their Creator, or who refuse to even consider the possibility of one when confronted with mountains, and mountains of evidence. They essentially sink to the level of object and idol worship, and when you think of it, they basically take a poly-theism viewpoint at that!!! Do you remember as you went through elementary school, how the concept of mono-theism was a concept considered a huge step in civilization and was, in fact one of the basic concepts that indicated advanced civilizations.   Well the wacko left seems to be going backwards. They now worship multiple gods depending on which sect of the religion of environmentalism you're in. It might be the "save the ocean sect", or the "save the wetland sect", or the "save the forest sect". You name it…they all have their own god.

Anyway, I got a little off track by bringing the environmental wacko's into this "Loon Moment", but I can't help it because guys like me represent a primary target for these groups. And why you ask? Let's see, I'm pretty sure it's because I believe in a God that created the universe, our planet and everything on it. I believe He made all the other creatures of this earth both for us to enjoy, AND for us to harvest responsibly when we need to. Therefore I hunt for their precious bird gods and I fish for their sacred fish gods in the streams, rivers, lakes and oceans of our planet. I believe in a God whose hidden his hand in the things around us; in nature, in the cosmos, in everything natural, and He didn't exactly go out of his way to make it hard for us to find Him. My God, my mother used to make it harder for me to find my Easter basket when I was a kid than God has tried to hide his presence in nature and in the universe. Yeah, she would hide it on the roof when I was five years old and then wonder why I hadn't gotten a ladder out of the garage and climb up on the roof to find it. And of course, she would set my sister's baskets out somewhere they'd trip over it as they were getting out of their beds. It's a good thing my mother doesn't listen to the show. At least she tells me she doesn't listen; I hope she's not listening today.

Anyway, those where the things I was thinking about as I sat out on a peaceful northern Wisconsin lake last week, searching for the elusive muskellunge and watching God's heavenly bodies rise into the evening sky. I dare anyone to gaze into the cosmos, or watch the sun, or the moon rise over some calm blue waters, anywhere - I dare you to do as God told us all to do; look to nature to see His hand. If you do it with an open mind and an open heart, I guarantee you'll find the Hand of our Creator. And that is the "Loon Moment" for today.

From the "Loon Moment" – November 4, 2006

Here's what I would have like to have added:

Wake up you morons, before it's too late! Exactly how self-absorbed do you have to be not to notice that God is amongst us; everywhere. How many times a day do you need to deny his existence so you can go about your daily life, day in and day out, breaking everyone of his laws and commandments? How many daily self-deceptions and rationalizations do you need a day to keep from seeing the obvious truth that we are created by a God who wants only for us to know him and obey him?

It's impossible for any truly aware person to deny the existence of God. We simply need to create cover for our sins and our poor behavior, so we use our God-given false intellect to create the bizarre rationalizations we need to do so - period. And in order to do that, it's a little problematic to acknowledge there's a God watching over your shoulder all the time. It's far easier just to deny Him.

I'm keeping my comments on this one pretty short. I don't want to get too preachy here because after all, I'm not exactly a perfect example of God's creation on a day to day basis myself. But one thing's for certain, for every instance of personal failure, for every weakness I'm unable to overcome and for every single time I'm just simply obstinate and disobedient towards my Creator, I worry like hell now. I'm thinking a few more of my liberal friends should do the same.

Scott Franz – July 2007

Four
"Save the Pigeons"

It's once again time for what has affectionately come to be known as "The Loon Moment". I know I often explain what the "Loon Moment" is all about, but that's for the benefit of new listeners who may be joining us for the first time.

The "Loon Moment" is a time in the show where I share with you and, I also welcome you to share with me, some of the many experiences we've all had in the outdoors and in experiencing nature. The "Loon Moment" can be just about anything. It can be about a fishing experience, or a quiet tranquil moment you've had in the outdoors; it can be about time spent with pals around a campfire, or a sunset shared with a wife, or child or another loved one. But in the end, the one thing in common all "Loon Moments" share is either a greater appreciation for the beauty of nature and the outdoors, or it presents a larger life lesson learned from those outdoor experiences.

I've got to tell you that there are some exceptions to this rule, because, well, because it's actually more of a guideline than a rule. And today's "Loon Moment" is one of those exceptions.

This story goes back to my days when I was working as a city forester. Although my title was "City Forester", you've got to remember that as a city employee, I was very often asked to perform duties which went, WAY, WAY beyond that of caring for the city's trees. And this story is about one of those cases.

Before I get started, I think you need to know that I'm a big animal lover. I qualify that by saying I'm not a PETA styled animal lover, not a "We're just like all other animals and we're all equal" type of animal lover, but a normal animal lover. I think you all know what I'm talking about, because by now you should know that I love to hunt and fish and, you're probably aware as well that I believe we humans, have dominion over the other creatures of the earth; meaning, in layman's terms, we get to harvest and eat them if we so desire.

I want to continue to reinforce the notion I'm a huge animal lover before I get into the meat of this story. As you know, I've owned dogs all of my adult life and you've heard me tell stories of my dog "Buckshot". To tell you the truth, next to humans, and they're really only running a close second at that, dogs are my favorite animal on the planet earth. I mean who can't love dogs. They're always there for you, no matter what kind of mood you're in; they're always happy to see you. I mean they are just great creatures all the way around.

So one more time I want to preface this story by making sure that you know I'm an animal lover, and because I don't want you to ever think that I could take any joy or pleasure in the pointless killing of any animal. I can't stand to see injured animals or animals suffering and I genuinely like <u>most</u> animals.

Now with all that being said and cleared up, you've got to understand the animal kingdom is a big place and not all animals are on equal footing in my book, and not all animals generate in me the same kind of feelings. For example, I think we can all agree that insects are in the animal kingdom and yet they hardly endear themselves to us as they bite, sting and otherwise annoy the heck out of us. For me, an awful lot of reptiles also fall into this same category. I just don't get all mushy and sad if I happen to see a snake that's been run over by a car, in the same way I would go.....AWWWW...if you happen to see a dog or some other animal in the same condition.

Now one of the more confusing animal groups for me, at least from an emotional standpoint, is birds. Who can fail to be inspired by the great birds of prey like eagles and ospreys? And who doesn't love to see hawks and falcons as they soar effortlessly over the tree tops. There are all kinds of birds I really like, and in case you're thinking I only like the majestic birds of prey, I also like robins and sparrows and, oh heck, I can't even name them all, all that I really like that is.

But THEN...There're the birds that one could care less about and which you don't really get all emotional about when they fly into buildings, or crash into plate glass windows or the grill of your car. Situated very squarely in this latter group of birds is the pigeon.

Now one day I'm out inspecting trees and I get a call from the forestry office about a bird stuck in a tree. Now I'm thinking to myself, "of course it's in a tree, it's a bird; where else would it be?" But anyway, I suggest to the dispatcher perhaps this was more of a situation for animal control officers than it was for a city forester, but apparently all of those officers were very busy elsewhere with really dangerous animals or something, like lions or tigers or bears, Oh My...

So I drive to the address I was given; it was very nearby a grammar school and there standing around this tree was an enormous crowd of concerned mothers, teachers and children, all standing in a circle around this tree. They were craning their necks and straining to get a better view of this bird; a pigeon that actually had managed to get itself stuck in a tree.

What had happened was this bird somehow had gotten its foot wrapped around what looked like mono-filament fishing line, and the other end of the line had wrapped around a tree limb; the result was essentially a pigeon on a leash, located about 40 feet up in the air in the tree.

I guess I was seen as the cavalry in this situation, because when I rolled up to the scene, I immediately got swarmed by the concerned group of onlookers who wanted the pigeon saved from its present predicament. I listened to all of their pleas and suggestions as to how to save this pigeon on a string. They ranged from suggesting I divert a bucket truck to the site, to calling the fire department's hook and ladder, neither of which I was prepared to do for a stuck pigeon. I finally got talked into personally making a rescue attempt.

Now I've already explained that I really hate pigeons and I couldn't have cared less about this particular pigeon's fate, but with all those sad faces looking up at me and their relentless pleadings for help, I decided to do my good deed for the day and rescue the pigeon.

I went back to my truck and got out a rope and saddle and start climbing into the tree for the rescue attempt. Now the higher I get in the tree and the closer I get to the pigeon, the greater the anticipation rises in the crowd below. I'm telling you, it was something you could really actually feel....

Finally, after a few minutes of climbing, I get as close to this bird as I possibly can, but the problem was this: At that height in the tree, the limbs were so small that I couldn't walk out on them far enough to get close enough to the pigeon without having a branch break out from under me. So after thinking for a minute, I finally decided I could still maneuver myself just a little closer; maybe close enough to the bird to reach out and cut him free with the some hand pruners, which I happened to be carrying with me. So I struggled and I maneuvered and eventually I got close enough to the bird so IF I reached as far as I could to cut the little twig the bird was attached to, it could fly free. Now the problem was that the bird was still going to have the line around its foot and would now be dragging a small amount of twig with him or her as well.

The situation was what it was and I decided it was worth the risk. There was no way I was going to get any closer, and I had to make an executive decision right then and there. So, I cut the little twig and the bird that was now flapping around like a madman at the end of this line was set free.

The very second I cut the bird free, it flew off in a rush and immediately a huge cheer went up from the gathered multitudes under the tree. And I've got to tell you, at the moment that bird flew free of its trap, you've never heard such a sigh of relief and so many sounds of excitement and joy.

Unfortunately, the joy and excitement was extremely short lived because of what happened next. As the bird flew off in a flurry of flapping wings and to the sounds of cheering and clapping, it headed right towards a lamppost that was located on the corner of the street. As it sped past the post, which happened to be the concrete aggregate type, with a lot of little bumps on it, the line the bird was still dragging behind it caught on the aggregate of the lamppost, at which point, the bird flew in ever, small and smaller circles as the line wrapped around the post. It was kind of like a tether ball wrapping around the tether pole, if that's what you call them (tether poles?) and this activity culminated with the bird smacking into the light pole at about MACH 1; the concussive effect killing it instantly.

Now of course this all happened in a split second and the roars and the cheers were still going on as the pigeon met the end of the line, both figuratively and literally, the cheers of joy and the sounds of excitement immediately becoming a collective sigh of despair.

You know I try hard to find a moral, or some life lesson during this segment of the show, and I know there's got to be a lesson or a moral in this story somewhere; but I've got to tell you I'm really struggling here to find one. Maybe it's something about how we should go out of our way to help, even if we don't like or agree with those we're helping. Or maybe it's about trying to show a little more compassion now and then, even for those in situations we don't truly understand or can relate too, or maybe, oh golly, I don't know, I'm truly struggling here...

I generally don't have to struggle so hard to find a lesson in my stories, but remember, I warned you upfront. I've already explained I've never been a big pigeon lover to begin with and I really felt I made a heroic effort to save the darn bird anyway. And I've got to tell you, the end of this pigeon, reminded me of the endings I used to see on Saturday morning cartoons and I had to stifle my laughter until I thought I was going to explode inside. It truly was a Wile E. Coyote moment from a visual point of view. So I've got nothing, absolutely nothing. No moral or lesson that goes along with this story, or if there is one, you're going to have to come up with it yourself. I hope you have more success than me. And that is the "Loon Moment" for today.

From -The "Loon Moment" – January 6, 2007

Here's what I would have like to have added:

I hope I wasn't too hard on pigeons in this broadcast. Immediately after it aired, I had a caller into the show who reminisced fondly about the good times he had with his elderly Italian grandfather who raised carrier pigeons. I had to admit that perhaps I'd judged the entire pigeon group a little too harshly. After all, his loving memories of raising and caring for his grandfather's pigeons and spending hours with him were the very essence of what the "Loon Moment" was all about. How could I deny him just because they happened to involve a species of bird we commonly refer to in the Chicago area as "flying rats"? I just couldn't. I probably had the only truly genuine pigeon lover, in a five county area, perhaps even in the station's entire three state listening area, calling into my show. If it would have been a PETA nut-job calling in, I could've had a field day with it and it would have been great radio. Just my luck!

Speaking of PETA, I recently found out that they kill more dogs and cats each year than a bad North Korean cuisine restaurant. So much for the fuzzy warm pictures of pandas and grizzly bears; they couldn't give a damn. They're all about fundraising; pure and simple and they absolutely aggravate the living hell out of me.

They never miss an opportunity to raise money and if you notice, they're never saving any ugly animals. See how much money you can raise with a "Save the Warthog" campaign. I hate to admit it, but I was listening to a "vegan" radio show today on Air America. I know, but it was for research; if you don't listen to these idiots, you can't get a real idea of how loony they really are. Anyway, they guy on the show was a true believer in animal rights whose job was with an investigative unit of some government agency. He basically said without naming any names that PETA, as an organization, jumped on every bandwagon, of every legitimate animal rights case for the purpose of fundraising; even though they had nothing at all to do with the case and couldn't influence it if they wanted to. They simply used the exposure of the case to raise funds, misleading prospective donors that their contributions would help prosecute that specific case. What a bunch of frauds.

I proudly proclaim myself as a carnivore and I'm glad to be exactly where I am in the food chain. I would probably even go cannibal if we only harvested PETA members. I hear they taste like chicken.

Scott Franz – July 2007

Five
"Give God His Props"

Well it's once again that time in the show for what has now become known as the "Loon Moment". It is by far my favorite segment of the show, because it's an opportunity for me to share some of the experiences I've had in the great outdoors, and more importantly, some of the realizations I've come to and some of the discoveries I've made as a result of those moments.

I don't generally have to think very hard to prepare for the "Loon Moment"; they just come to me. I'll sit down to prepare for the show and specifically for the "Loon Moment" and something just triggers an experience or moment stored in my brain. It might be an old photo, maybe a smell, maybe some artifact I have in my office, it could be anything, and from there.....bam....a "Loon Moment" I can share with you springs into my mind. But as I sat down to prepare for today's show, I was troubled by the fact that nothing, absolutely nothing was coming into my head. And as I said earlier, generally speaking, I don't have to put in any effort at all into a "Loon Moment".

Now I've got to tell you, I've had literally thousands of experiences I could share with you about the outdoors and nature; real life experiences, and it would take months to tell them all to you. BUT, because I try to end each "Loon Moment" with a little lesson learned, I came to realize what was troubling me as I tried to prepare for today's show. Very simply it was the fact that I haven't really learned that many <u>different</u> lessons from all of my experiences. I mean I've learned a lot of outdoor skills, and I know how to do a lot of things, and I've had just a plethora of great and special personal moments; moments that brought me closer to people I love and care about. But ultimately, ultimately, I haven't learned a great number of different meaningful life lessons.

You might be asking yourself at this point, where exactly is he going with this? What's the point then? Well it's your lucky day, because I'm going to tell you and I'm going to tell you something important. What's happened in those thousands of moments, what's happened in those endless experiences in the outdoors, is basically this: It's been the re-enforcement of the same lesson, or more specifically, the same discovery, over and over, and over again. Not a new lesson every time, not a new discovery every time, but the same one, time and time again, only in a different way. It's a discovery and a realization that makes me, what you know I've often referred to myself as, a self-described "conservative environmentalist". This would be opposed to the mindless, godless environmental whackos, or the Druids, as Ann Coulter would call them. These would be the Pagan "Mother Earth" believers I'm referring to. And the lesson, that discovery that sets me apart from that crowd is very simply this: All we ever need to do if we want to see the Hand of our Creator is to look about us in nature.

Look to the birds of the sky, look to the lilies of the field, look to the vastness of the ocean and the endlessness of space. Look at the planets and look at the multitude of stars. Look in those places, and if you look hard, and with an open mind and heart, you will find GOD. At the very same moment you will realize both your absolute insignificance, AND your monumental significance. What a huge contradiction, and yet it's so very true.

How exactly can we realize at the very same moment how insignificant we are as individuals and yet how monumentally significant we are, as individuals? It seems like such a huge contradiction, but in reality, it's not. When you look and find our Creator, our God in the natural things about us, and realize that HE created all of those things with HIS purpose in mind, right down to the tiniest creature, the most minute organism, all of them serving a very distinct purpose, HIS purpose, well then, it's very simple to come to the conclusion we too <u>MUST</u> have a purpose as well; a role to play that is preordained by our Creator.

We are not mere accidents, we are not the product of chance, we did not rise from some pre-biotic soup as a group of cell that just happened to evolve into human beings, and as insignificant as we may feel in the great wheel of life sometimes, we are every bit as important in GOD's unseen plan as the mightiest person on the planet. All of us are equally important and we hold equal significance in the eyes of our Creator. So I guess in the end, we're pretty damn significant in our seeming insignificance.

I guess I'm getting a little philosophical here for a radio talk, but what I'm telling you is simply this: look to the natural world and you will find our Creator, our GOD; and when you do, just acknowledge HIM and HIS work. Acknowledge the things you simply know in your being to be true. You've known it from the time before your brain got cluttered up with education by the godless left-wing academia, and the pagan, druid environmentalists. Simply become a child again and take the time to truly marvel at, and simply acknowledge what you know intuitively. Things cannot be created from nothing, except by God. All things we know and see then, are created by our GOD and were created for a purpose.

In the final analysis we all intuitively know this, and yet science and educators commit the ultimate sin of pride and arrogance in refusing to acknowledge it to be true. They spend all their time and effort trying to create scenarios to explain away a God whose presence is simply undeniable. All we need do is look at the things HE's created, and I might add, has created for us to use. That's right, use. The oil, the timber, the gold, the oceans, the fish in them, they are there for us to use, not to be on an equal footing with. And they are there for us to enjoy, immensely enjoy. Personally, I think all He really wants from us anyway is just a little tip of the hat, a little acknowledgment and appreciation for what He's given us - a few props, so to speak, and a heartfelt thank you.

So that's the lesson I keep learning time and time again from my experiences in the outdoors. It's simply this: I was created for a purpose along with the sun, and the stars and the moon and the trees and the shrubs and the grubs; and that lesson gets reinforced with every sunset, every meteor shower, every lightning storm, every one of God's displays that were created specifically for us to recognize and ACKNOWLEDGE His presence and His works.

Now don't get too hung up with trying to figure out God's purpose in life for you, it just ends up leading to more sins of pride and arrogance. Because the human side of us always wants to do great things and we want to raise ourselves to the level of God himself. If you're a liberal you generally prefer to lower all of mankind to the same significance as the spotted owl, or the yellow-throated screech pigeon, I don't know. But I do know that our real purpose in life is simply to acknowledge and know our God; appreciate Him and thank Him, not to necessarily figure out his plan for us. The only thing we have in common with the single cell bacteria is that we have a God given purpose and that generally, we are as totally unaware of that purpose as the bacteria. So we have a purpose in God's plan and we'll never have a clue what that purpose really is. I'm not sure, but I doubt if we're ever really intended to know.

So the next time you have a "Loon Moment", maybe it's a smile shared between you and your child while fishing, or maybe a shared sunset with your wife, or maybe it's a moment when you feel the true bond of friendship with some pals while out in nature, or maybe it's just a moment alone looking up at the stars on a clear night. At that moment, just get simple again, be a child again and acknowledge your Creator. You might want to say a little thank you to Him as well. And that is the Loon Moment for Today.

From the "Loon Moment" – Dec.16, 2006

Here's what I would have like to have added:

Actually, in this particular case, I said exactly what I wanted to say. The only people that would have been offended by the above broadcast would be the mindless, godless left wing. They rarely listened anyway and if they did, it was by accident.

Scott Franz – August 2007

Six
"Campfires & Clouds"

Well here we are again. It's that time of the show known as the "Loon Moment, and as you know by now, it's personally my favorite segment of the show. It's a time in the show when I, or more accurately we, can reflect a little about nature, or maybe things we've experienced in nature, or lessons learned because of those experiences in nature. Sometimes it's a humorous story that involves the outdoors, or sometimes it's about a moment shared in nature with someone who's very special to us, and sometimes, even sometimes it can be a about a tragic story about just how little control we have over nature, or just how lethal and forceful nature can be whether we're prepared for it or not.

But today's "Loon Moment" is about campfires and clouds. You heard me right, campfires and clouds.

I think I've mentioned in a very recent "Loon Moment" about how powerful a memory trigger our sense of smell is and it was another one of those triggers that got me going for today's "Loon Moment". I was actually trying out one of the Northwood's candles we're giving out on the show today. Believe it or not and pardon the commercial plug, but we don't offer anything for sale on our website that's not "Green Hour Approved", which means I have to know it's a good product through first-hand experience. Anyway, I had one of the Northwood's candles burning and I had chosen the campfire scented candle. Now you know, like a lot of men who retain a lot of boy in them, I'm a nut as it is about burning things. I have this huge outdoor fireplace in my back yard and I'm always outside burning logs or scrap wood, and I do it for the very simple reason that I love the smell of a camp fire. I get some real blazers going from time to time too. Boys will be boys, eh? So anyway, I've got this candle lit and the scent of a campfire is in the air. I mean it really smells like a campfire and it starts to trigger memories for me.

I don't know about you, but for me, sitting around a campfire either alone or with a group of friends is probably one of the more pleasant experiences one can have on this planet. There's certainly something very mesmerizing about a campfire or even a fire in the fireplace. There's just something that draws your attention to the flame and the glow of the embers, and if you stare at it long enough, you can see images in the fire and the embers that start to resemble things. It's a lot like lying on your back and staring up at clouds on a clear blue day. Pretty soon the clouds start to look like things, instead of just looking like, well clouds. And the same thing begins to happen, at least to me, around a campfire. There's just something about clouds and campfires that seems to free the imagination.

Anyway, I smelled the smell that exactly replicates a campfire and I start to think about some of the pleasant times I've had sitting around a campfire with family or friends. And as I'm doing so I've got the television on in the background and the movie "Dances with Wolves" is on. The scene playing is where Kevin Costner is sitting inside a teepee with a big group of his Sioux friends right after the big buffalo hunt is over, and they keep making him tell a story about the hunt, and they keep feeding him, and feeding him, and they're all smiling and laughing, and the glow of the fire in the center of the teepee is reflecting on all of their faces - it's just a great scene. It's a scene about a small group of people who all care about each other, and more importantly about people who all depend on each other and love each other. They're all sharing this very fine, intimate moment around the warm glow of a campfire, with full bellies and big smiles. What could be better?

The thing that struck me most about this whole scene taking place on the screen, particularly as I took in the scent from my Northwood's candle, is that we simply need and could all use, a little more campfire time. Certainly we need more as families and probably as a society as a whole. It's really hard to be angry or mad, or continue to hold a grudge against someone when you're fat, well fed, happy, cozy warm, and sitting around the warm glow of a communal fire. It's actually almost impossible. All of your angst seems to melt away under those circumstances, and why shouldn't they? With all of our basic needs as human beings fulfilled, we generally only need or seek one other thing, and that's the love, companionship and fellowship of other humans.

I think sometimes we search too often in life for so much more than we really need. And we've become a society driven by people and companies who are absolutely expert in creating in us desires having nothing to do with our basic needs in life. We have become such a consumer driven society and we constantly want more and more, and after we get it, it tends to feed on itself and we crave even more. Generally, I'd have to say these cravings and desires for more are simply harmful to us as human beings, and take us farther and farther away from the things in life that truly make us happy.

I know this cycle has happened to me, and I doubt I'm that much weirder than you are, so it's probably happened to you as well. How many times have you used this argument on yourself to justify acquiring something else you really didn't need? The argument in your brain goes something like this: "As soon I have (name the object of your desire), then everything will be OK". Surprisingly, as soon as you have that object of your desire, you find that everything is still not OK and you replace that object of desire with a new one. It's a classic cycle, and it's one that the marketers and advertising people count on; and time and time again, we fall for it. We're such suckers.

The sooner we realize that objects don't make us happy and the acquisition of objects won't bring us true happiness, the better off we are. And when that realization hits, we start to focus on the things in life that really matter. We stop trying to acquire things, and begin to give, and that's when we can truly achieve happiness.

I've tried hard to teach this lesson to my children, but it's a tough one, especially when I have to try to keep remembering and fighting the self gratification urge myself. We are fighting a battle against a powerful foe and one that has a great battle plan, and a powerful ally within us all, Greed. Just look at the scenes in the news the past few weeks where people are beating each other and shooting each other, just to be the first to purchase a limited number of hot toys or games at Walmart. We've got people literally camping out to make sure they are first in line for the latest game or toy. Now I'm wondering to myself; just how good can you feel about yourself after acquiring your Playstation "X-treme" (or whatever the heck the name of that toy was that people were lining up for on Black Friday), if you've had to beat the crap out of some person to acquire it.

It seems I've gotten a long way away from clouds and campfires, but I had to because the larger point had to be made, and that point is that in the end, we all leave this earth with exactly what we came into with; absolutely zilch. And while we're here, we better focus on what's important and forget about the stupid, endless pursuit of objects, objects we'll only become slaves to anyway.

So as we get nearer and nearer to Christmas, that time of year when the marketers and ad men appeal to us with their most psychologically devious schemes to trigger our greed and fuel our desires, think about who and what's really important in your life and take a little time to schedule some campfire time with them. Bask in the warm glow of that campfire with your friends and family and try to give to each and every one of them the thing they really desire the most, some of your precious time. And that is the "Loon Moment" for Today.

From the "Loon Moment" – Dec. 9, 2006

Here's what I would have like to have added:

Once again, I didn't really feel the heavy hand of the censor or big brother upon me as I did the above "Moment". If anything, my only restraint was not wanting to elaborate and announce to the entire world my own shortcomings and failures as a father and husband; my failure to give more of myself and my time to my wife and family. Throughout life it's always so easy to justify the time you rob from your loved ones. We tell ourselves it's our duty to provide for them as best as we can and in the course of doing so, we rob them of what they need most from us.

As my father likes to say, we all have to step off the bus one of these days. When it's your turn or my turn for that matter to take that step, will you feel good about how many and what kind of memories you've given to those we leave behind? The fact I have to still wonder about it, keeps me praying I still have enough time to leave more. And that is the "Loon Moment" for today.

Scott Franz – March 2007

Seven
"God Within Us"
(Buckshot's First Hunt)

Well it's that time again in our show for what we have now affectionately come to call the "Loon Moment". We always do this segment right at the beginning the second hour of the show, so for those of you who are new to the "Green Hour", first and foremost welcome, I'm glad you're here and secondly, I'll take a moment to clue you in to what the "Loon Moment" is all about.

During the "Loon Moment" I always like to share with you, AND of course, I look forward to you sharing with me, some of the experience we've had enjoying the outdoors. It can be about pretty much anything; any outdoor experience at all but generally speaking, whatever the experience, it's usually one that's made you pause and reflect – at least a little. And it's usually one that makes you realize just how much you appreciate either that moment; or perhaps the person you're sharing it with, or how you've come to some greater realization through experiencing it. For me, my "Loon Moments" always tend to make me reflect a little about the grander scheme of things, but that's just me.

Now last week I think I mentioned my new dog "Buckshot" had his first outing as a bird dog; his very first hunt and I want to tell you about it during today's "Loon Moment". Of course, the whole experience just got me thinking about something else, something much larger, which again of course, is the real point of today's "Loon Moment". So if you want to know what that point is, you'll just have to listen to the whole story. So stay with me.

Three of my buddies and me went off the Friday before Christmas to try out this new Hunt Club out in Freeport, Illinois. My friend Jack, the famous "musky killer" had set up the whole outing. Now in the process of setting things up he had arranged a guide and some bird dogs, but had asked if it was alright if we brought our own dog as well; meaning my dog "Buckshot". He let them know that "Bucky" was just a "little new" to the game and not very well trained as a bird dog yet. At the time he set up the outing, the operators of the club said sure, absolutely no problem; bring your dog.

So we drive out in the pouring rain and we're wondering if we're even going to be able to get the hunt in because of the weather. Miraculously, just as we get there, the rain stops and the hunt is on. But as we're going over some of the club rules with the folks that run the place, they kind of changed their mind about allowing outside dogs to participate and told us that they didn't want a new dog working with the hunting dogs they were providing. So I was a little bummed out, but then they offered up an alternative and suggested that I could hunt with the guide for a while and then take my dog to an adjacent field and work with him. Well that sounded pretty good to me, so everything was OK and the hunt was on.

I've got to tell you, for me one of the great joys of bird hunting is watching the dogs work. Don't get me wrong, I like the end result and my family enjoyed a fantastic pheasant dinner (I'll share the recipe with you some other time), but it's just great to see well trained bird dogs work during a hunt. If you ever want to see an animal in his or her true element and truly enjoying themselves, then you've got to see a great bird dog working a field for pheasant or quail or chucker or whatever.

So we hunted with the guide's two dogs; one was a German shorthair, who was a little inexperienced himself, but the other was a very, very, enthusiastic English Labrador who I thought was just a fantastic dog and did great.

I'm a big believer that there really isn't that much to training bird dogs; it comes pretty naturally to them. They only need to get used to the scent of the birds and to learn and realize that they're there to find that scent and not out for play time. So after a couple of hours and a bunch of birds, it was finally "Buckshot's" turn to hunt.

Now I'd been working with him a little, not very much, but as soon as I let him out of his crate and we started walking that field he instantly became a "bird dog". Not only was he a bird dog, but he was perhaps the happiest creature on the planet during the next hour and half as he worked that field looking for birds. And man alive, I've got to tell you, he did just great; and that's when I started to realize something.

It seems to me, the reason he did so well was because he was just being the quintessential bird dog. His true nature came out the minute he was out in that field and he didn't have to think. He didn't need to be trained to do anything; he just had to be himself. He just had to let his true nature come out and all was fine with the world. How beautiful is it that dogs, or any other animal for that matter, don't have any conflict within them? They don't have a split nature; you'll never see a schizophrenic dog. They have only one nature, one personality, the dog nature, and that's when it hit me again.

The problem we have as human beings is we have two distinct natures; not one like the other animals and it's the conflict of those two natures that causes all of our problems. You see as human beings we are endowed with the nature of our Creator, call it what you will. You can call it our soul, you can call it our spirit, it doesn't matter what you call it; the fact is the phrase "We are all made in the image of our Creator" means that we have a spiritual or god-like nature inherent in all of us. We have it, no other creature does, and it's what sets us apart from all the other creatures of the earth.

Now I don't care a hoot what PETA tells you, apes don't have it, no matter how human they sometimes look. Dogs don't have it, cows don't have it; only human beings have it and only humans are made in the image of God, and each and every one of us carries with us the true nature and essence of God. Actually, God Himself resides in each of us and our God nature, or God within us gives us another thing that animals don't have - The moral compass that comes with our God nature; it's called a conscience. Now that's both the good news and, for some of us, the bad news as well.

Now the really bad news is we also carry with us our human nature, and that's the nasty little thing that's always bumping into our God nature. Our human nature is kind of base and vulgar and for those of you who are strict interpreters of the bible, we acquired it when Eve took a bite of the forbidden fruit and then conned Adam into a little taste. All of a sudden our eyes were opened to all that was in conflict with our Creator and God within us. In addition, our eyes were opened to all that is, and all there ever will be to tempt us away from it.

What a rotten turn of events that was for mankind. I suppose it had to happen, because if it hadn't, we really wouldn't be creatures of choice, and in the end, everything boils down to that anyway. Every single day we have to choose to either follow our God-nature as we are intended to do, or let our human nature rule and be in conflict with our Creator. Every day of our lives we have this unbelievable battle going on between our two natures. It sure doesn't seem right or fair to be saddled with this ongoing, raging, conflict within, does it? Well, I guess it's right, but that doesn't keep it from being a royal bummer.

Back to the hunt. So I'm watching the dogs work the field and I'm thinking to myself, man look how happy those critters are. They're just happy being dogs and being true to their nature. There's no conflict; there's no guilt; there's no questioning the meaning of their existence, there's no internal tug-of war going on, there's nothing like that. They are happy just being as God created them; simply existing as dogs and being true to their nature.

Now the hunt was over and "Buckshot" and I had a great day together and I was so happy and proud of him because he had done so well. But really, when it came down to it, he hadn't had to work at it all. He just had to be himself and I was just a little jealous of him; just for a second. And the reason I was jealous was because he didn't need to put forth any effort to let his true nature come out; not today, and he won't have to put forth any effort the next time or the time after that, or the one after that, because he'll always have only one true nature, that of a dog.

I one the other hand will always be stuck with my rotten human nature and the inherent battle between it and my God-like nature, which we are all intended to **Choose** to be our dominant nature, and which if we do, can snuff out and kill the vile human nature within us.

The next time you hear the animal rights people or PETA tell you that we're no different from any other creature on this planet, think to yourself if any other animal species has the heavy burden of a conscience, or the struggle with two completely polar opposite natures, the daily struggle to choose between our good, spiritual, God-like nature or our base, vile human nature.

If you're struggling to answer this question, I'll help you out and give you the answer. **It's an unqualified NO**. There is no struggle, there is no conscience; no matter how cute they are, no matter what faces they make, no matter what human-like antics they pull off, the answer is still a resounding **NO**.

It would certainly be simpler if we only had one true nature like my dog "Buckshot" or like any other cute little critter. In one way, we can be a little jealous of them and in the simplicity of their existence. **But** because we have something that they will never have, the ability to <u>Choose</u>; either to let our God-nature take over our existence in the place of our base human nature and, well.... Well it's because of this choice we have something above all other creatures, the ability to know and to have a personal relationship with our Creator, our GOD.

If we choose to let our human nature rule we can gain all kinds of human rewards, kind of like the tasty little dog treats I gave "Buckshot" after the hunt. But, if we choose our God-like nature, we can't and shouldn't expect a whole lot of rewards just now. Our doggie treats, so to speak, come much, much, later and are not of this world. And that is the "Loon Moment" for today.

From the "Loon Moment" – Dec. 30, 2006

Here's what I would have like to have added:

If I left anything out from this moment, it had nothing to do with what I could, would, or should have said on the public airwaves. I sure hope the listeners and readers of this story can absorb it without figuring out just how personally conflicted I am, and have always been, on a day to day basis throughout my life. It's a little embarrassing to admit. Does anyone else struggle? Am I the only "non-Mother Theresa" on the planet or does being a good Christian, follower of Jesus and child of God come easily to everyone but me? Based on my observations, I'm guessing a few of you struggle as well.

Of course then, there're a lot of people who don't struggle at all. They just don't give a damn; they're called liberals.

Putting Christianity to practice in your daily life and doing everything our Lord tells us to do is personally something of a bitch for me, and something which neither comes naturally or easily. And to tell you the truth, I'm a little hacked off about the whole choice thing that God gave us. Life would be a lot simpler without it and if I wanted to get rid of the whole nagging issue altogether, I could just change my voter registration card to read Democrat and presto, no more stressing out about right and wrong. Unfortunately, that's not in the cards for me and if you're reading this book; it's probably not a viable option for you either. How about a deal? I'll include you in my prayers and you include me in yours and we'll just keep struggling to make the right choices together. We won't always succeed. There's only been one perfect being ever to walk this planet and neither you nor I are HIM.

God Bless You – Scott Franz April 2007

Eight
"Gifts From Above"

Here we are again. It's time for the "Loon Moment". Maestro Julio may we have the now patented "Loon Moment" mood music please. Thank you. Ah - there's absolutely nothing like the call of the loon to calm you down once you've gotten yourself wound up a bit.

When I was thinking about today's show and specifically, when I was thinking about what I was going to talk about during today's "Loon Moment", I was getting pulled in a lot of different directions. I really could have gone in a lot of different ways for today's moment.

For example, I've literally been bombarded since last Tuesday with gleeful blast e-mails from the Sierra Club about how great things are going to be for the country's environment now that the Democrats will soon be in charge. And of course, I had already been bombarded in the days before the election by the same kind of blast e-mails just loaded with nifty little one-liner promises from Democratic candidates, which I think were actually supposed to convince those on the loony left that something VERY, VERY dramatic would actually change for the environment if the democrats were in charge of things; and change overnight. I have to admit, I actually love those one-liners and sound bites and I think the guys who write them happen to be very talented. They're specifically designed to make as many promises, to as many different factions as you can appease; all crammed into a single sentence or sound bite.

I'm thinking I should personally go into the business of writing sound bites for candidates running specifically on environmental issues. I think I'd be good at it if I practiced a little. So I'm going to give it a whirl. Bear with me now, I'm just warming up and practicing. Here's what I would write or say if I was running for, I don't know, say Governor of Illinois. If any of you politicians are listening and I hear any of this come out of your mouths in the future, I want to warn you that all material on the "Green Hour" is copyrighted, trademarked, service marked and patents are pending. Ok, here's my environmental sound bite answering the question, "What would you do about pollution in Illinois?" --

"I'll work hard to develop initiatives, bi-partisan initiatives, which absolutely hold the promise of creating clean, renewable energy from thin air. Initiatives that clearly make cutting our ties to foreign oil a REAL possibility, not just an empty promise. And I'll propose legislation that will produce the jobs needed to create that clean, renewable energy, so everyone will get a bigger, fairer piece of the pie, with a scoop of ice cream on top; and they'll be able to make a decent living too, and not have to live under power lines like some of you poor working stiffs; because when we remove houses from under power lines, well, that'll reduce brain tumors too, which will lower health premiums and put even more money in your pockets. Illinois families will be able to send their kids to private schools if they want and we'll still have enough money to properly fund public

education so even the dumbest, dullest among our kids will not be left behind and forced to end up serving in the military (according to Sen. John Kerry); and we can bring our boys home from Iraq sooner and they can be good productive citizens here in Illinois, making cleaner, renewable energy for all Illinoisans" – Stand by. I'm out of breath. This is a lot harder than I thought. I've got to take a break.

As you can plainly see, I could have gotten myself all worked up about the environment, or the wacky left during today's "Loon Moment", or I could have gotten myself all angry and worked up about politics, but then I stopped and said to myself; Self, I said, the "Loon Moment" can be about a lot of things, but one thing it can't be is angry. Oh, perhaps it can be a little frightening at times, it can certainly be reflective and hopefully inspiring at times, and maybe once, maybe just once in a while I'll be able to dig down real deep and I'll even be able to make it a bit humorous; BUT, I cannot and will not desecrate a "Loon Moment" with even a hint or moment of anger.

So anyway, since I can't be or get angry during the "Loon Moment" and as I sat back and I thought about the ways I keep from getting angry these days; I'm sure you have your own tricks for this, but I thought I'd share mine with you as the point of today's moment. First of all, as a general rule, I just don't really get angry that often anymore. I generally only reach the level of regularly and almost permanently annoyed, but not angry. When I do start feeling myself cross the threshold and start getting close to the anger zone, I generally start to remind myself just how lucky a man I really am and how blessed in life I've really been. And I don't mean to say that I haven't been without my own trials and tribulations. I've had my share and I continue to have them as I speak to you, and they come at me in all of the different aspects of my life.

But a long time ago, I realized what very little control I had over my life and what little control we all have over our lives. I realized I'm not here to serve myself or to be in control of my own or anyone else's life, but that I and we are all here and are being used for a much higher purpose, one which neither you nor I will probably ever understand in our lifetimes. And because I'm not really in control, I know I can't really bring myself to joy or to happiness, or to be loved or to love. I can't bring myself to riches or to success or to exalt myself worldly; and for me to strive towards any of those purposes is really at direct cross purposes with the plan my Creator has intended for me.

Once I truly understood this, I came to realize that whatever joy and happiness I find in life, if only for the briefest moments, whatever love and friendship I've found in this world, whatever successes have come my way, well then, they were all truly gifts; gifts that had been given or made available specifically to or for me; and consequently, all things for which I should be very, very thankful.

With all these gifts each and every one of us is given every day of our lives, I dare you to try and stay mad, or angry, or resentful if you reflect for even a moment on how lucky you personally really are. And I double dare you to try and stay WORRIED for even a moment when once you realize that you are not in control of these fabulous gifts. Once you truly realize it and come to grips with it, what in the world is there to worry about? We all tend to scurry about this planet like little squirrels, worrying about our nest eggs and our nut count for the winter, or always thinking about tomorrow, tomorrow, tomorrow, tomorrow. Worse yet, we're thinking about the next big deal, or our retirement that's 20 years away, or the next vacation we want to take, the next thrill we want to experience, or whatever; all the time we're worrying about tomorrow, without a single one of us really <u>knowing</u> with any certainty whether or not we'll even be given that tomorrow. And so we seem to never be able stop looking into the future, because we so sure we can control the outcome of that future if only we diligently work this plan or follow these proven guidelines. While we're doing all that planning and scheming it's easy to completely miss out on today and ignore the very gifts we've been given today, this <u>very</u> day, because they seem insignificant when viewed in light of OUR grand plans. The gifts right in front of us, right here and right now, we refuse to fully cherish or enjoy as we're intended.

Now believe me; I'm not preaching to you. I guilty of the very thing I'm talking to you about all the time. I constantly get all caught up in myself and in all my plans, but I find I'm doing it less and less all the time, and I'm more and more grateful for whatever gifts God has given me today. And I've got to tell you, not a day goes by that I don't get something from the Big Guy; whatever that something is, whether it's a sunset, like the one I saw a couple of weeks ago while I was fishing, or whether it's the joy and the love I get from my wife, or my family and friends. There's always something, something in every single day that makes me feel very, very lucky and something else that <u>warns</u> me not to take them for granted, not for one single moment.

Once I figured out where these gifts really come from, and I'm thankful and consciously give thanks for them to their giver, I seem to keep getting them in greater and greater quantities. Now, there's a quiet voice in me that constantly whispers, share all these gifts and share them with everyone you come in contact with. It's really quite an amazing thing when you think about it. Has there ever been anything that you've truly cherished that you didn't want to share, that you wanted to keep all to yourself? The more you cherish it, I mean truly cherish it, the more you want to share it. That's just the way it works. If you're keeping something to yourself it's probably not very good for you. If you hoard anything, anything at all, it will most probably be your downfall.

So sit quietly for a few moments today and try to remember a time when you've smiled or a time when you were truly inspired, or when you felt true joy and happiness. When you do finally remember that time, I'll bet you'll remember it as a time or a moment you shared with someone else. Then think a little further today and try to find out what it is you truly cherish, truly cherish <u>today</u>. After you've found that thing, go find someone to share it with. I think you'll find that you're really giving yourself a tremendous gift and you'll realize how lucky and blessed you are this very day as well. And that, my friends is a true gift directly from our Creator to you; and this has been the "Loon Moment" for today.

From the "Loon Moment" – November 11, 2006

Here's what I would have like to have added:

I didn't add this postscript to the above until several years after it aired on the radio. My life has changed dramatically since that time, and by most people's yardsticks, it's changed for the worse. As I write this, I suspect a lot of lives are going to change, for a lot of people, in the years to come. I suspect they'll change in ways they'd never been able to anticipate or plan. And I'll be willing to bet the loss of control they'll feel will devastate some. Fortunately, many others will be fine.

Since the broadcast above, my health has deteriorated, I've been ruined financially, and I've got messes to in my life which will probably take the bulk of my remaining time on this planet to clean up. That being said, I haven't changed my opinions or beliefs one iota. If I was still on the air and could broadcast it again, I would try my best to make it even more forceful, more persuasive and if I could, more comforting to those going through or about to go through a similar time.

While my present situation and outlook for the future look dire by most human standards, I still consider myself the luckiest man on the planet. I truly do. I've been so blessed and showered with the kind of gifts I spoke of in my broadcast, that if I never received another, I'd have nothing to complain about – nothing at all. My bride of close to thirty years and I managed to raise four children. While I'd be hard pressed to call them all perfect, they've all turned *out pretty damned good and I couldn't be prouder about the way they all approach their lives. One of them has already presented me with another precious gift, my first grandchild. What a sheer joy she has been as I've struggled through some of my present day issues. I've received and continue to receive so many others, it would be impossible to list them all here. Sometimes, I've had to look a little harder to find them, but nevertheless, I get them.*

It's funny how the trials and tribulations of daily life, the loss of control of one's circumstances and the flushing of well laid plans down life's toilet can have different effects on different people. I suspect the people best prepared to deal with life altering events are those who long ago have relinquished control of their lives to GOD. Those that try and maintain control of those things which they'll never be able to control are in for the worst of it. They'll erroneously see the failure of their plans and the destruction of their dreams as a personal failure. Why, you ask? Because of the mistaken perception they were somehow in control of their lives; and it's hard to accept personal failure, no matter who you are.

No matter what happens in the years to come, don't forget to look for and be thankful for the gifts you receive from your Creator every day. Sometimes you'll have to look through the fog, or change the lenses a bit, or get past some of the tribulations or struggles you're going through. But trust me, if you truly look, you'll be able to find them. Be thankful for each and every one of them and give thanks where it belongs.   *Scott Franz – February 2009*

Nine
"Memories of Burning Leaves"

Well here we are again. It's time again in our show for the "Loon Moment". If you've been listening for any length of time you already know what the "Loon Moment" is about; and if you know what the "Loon Moment" is all about - well, you're doing better than I am, because it's another one of those segments in the show where I give myself an awful lot of latitude to go just about anywhere I want. Generally, it's a time when we can share an experience we've had in the great outdoors or in nature; an experience that tends to make us reflect just a little bit on something a little bigger and larger than the moment itself.

Now most of the moments I share with you during the "Loon Moment" are generally things that I've experienced somewhere in my distant past, but today's moment is just a little different, because today's "Loon Moment actually happened just the other day. It was Thanksgiving Day to be exact, but it so very much reminded me of the distant past.

Now I mentioned in the beginning of the show that I was down in central Illinois for Thanksgiving Day and I spent a good deal of the day outside. Mostly I was outdoors because it was such a beautiful day, but there was a secondary reason - my crazed Labrador retriever Buck. Let's just say he wasn't exactly the most welcome guest in a house with two Bichons. That is the name of those yappy little un-trainable dogs isn't it? Yes I'm sure of it, Bichons, that's it. Anyway, my dog was the designated villain of the day as he was upsetting the Bichons, so we spent a lot of time outside on Thursday. We couldn't and wouldn't cause so much anxiety with the yappy little Bichons or with my father-in-law for that matter if we were outside. It was a wonderful, beautiful day anyway, with sunshine and blue skies; so everything was fine by me.

I know I've heard somewhere your sense of smell is a powerful memory trigger, and as my dog and I were rather gleefully banished to the outdoors, I caught the smell of burning leaves. Ah….the smell of burning leaves. Now I don't know about you, but to me, it's one of the most wonderful smells known to mankind, and it just brought memories flooding back to me of my childhood days.

I know I'm not the only one who can remember back to the days when it was OK to burn leaves right in the street during the fall. It wasn't like it is today and it seems such a long time ago. These days you have to have your leaves out in the street by a certain day so that a 40 ton front-end loader can push them down to the end of the block and then load them into a huge dump truck to be carted off to God only knows where. I suppose they are properly composted and turned into something useful for mankind. I guess, I don't know for sure. But back then you could just rake your leaves into the street and burn them right there in the middle of the street, imagine that. The smell of those days was glorious.

Now back when I was a kid leaf burning was a great deal of fun in the neighborhood because, of course, you were never the only family burning leaves on any given day. There were generally all kinds of piles burning all up and down the street, and people were out and about, talking to each other over the burning piles. It was great fun for us kids and it was a time for the whole neighborhood to be outdoors. And of course, everyone had to stay out for a quite a while to watch the fires and make sure they were completely burnt out before they could go about other activities. It was a great time to catch up a little bit with each other and to chat up your neighbors.

On leaf burning days, all the kids in the neighborhood were out. We'd run from pile to pile and we'd get to rake a little and throw more leaves on the pile. The boys, of course, would start little sticks on fire and chase each other with the burning sticks, which of course would go out right away. We'd always get yelled at by one parent or another for doing it (it was one of those "You're going to put someone's eye out" kind of yells anyway – the kind you could generally ignore without getting into too much trouble), so we'd go down the block a little further and get yelled at again by another parent who hadn't seen us just moments before. All in all, it was just a good 'ole time. Kind of like a block party without the food.

Now I'm talking about all the great memories I had associated with the simple act of burning leaves in the fall, and It strikes me how much neighborhoods have changed since then, and how much we've really lost since then with all the damn rules and restrictions we're now bound by in today's day and age. I was trying to remember the reason that leaf burning got banned in the first place, however long ago that was. It must be decades by now since we've been able to do it. Was it a pollution thing or was it a fire safety thing that it got banned? I don't really remember the reason back then. Maybe it was both of those reasons; I really can't recall, but what struck me the other day as those smells brought back memories of cool fall days, blue skies, and that wonderful, wonderful smell, is that both of those reasons are BS anyway. I don't know about you, but for the life of me, I can never, ever, ever, remember a single case of somebody's house catching on fire from burning leaves in the street. I certainly can't remember anyone ever getting hurt or getting burned beyond recognition, or the forest preserves starting on fire from flying embers. I'm telling you, I can't ever remember a single bad thing happening because of people burning leaves in the street.

So I'm just guessing now, but if it wasn't a safety issue, it must have been a pollution issue, and somehow, somebody thought that all that smoke from the burning leaves must be adding to pollution levels. Yeah, I think that's right. That was it.

Now if it was a pollution issue, I know it couldn't have been linked to global warming back then, because at the time, if you're old enough to recall, the noted scientists of the day were far more concerned that we were about to experience another ice age (They've sure changed their tune in 40 years, haven't they). It could have been about smog or air quality, or something like that, which got me to thinking about the difference between then and now.

Back then, a couple of weekends a year, the leaves would be burned and a little smoke would get in the air. Not the bad kind of smoke mind you, not the smoke of the combustion engine, which gives off those nasty, horrible green house gases, the smoke we've all been taught to abhor. NO, it was the good smoke of natural organic matter being burned, like the smoke from a forest fire, or a controlled burn (It's OK to burn if you're saving a wetland or forest preserve or other ecologically sound reasons, just not to get those damn leaves off your street). So now, instead of the smoke from the burning piles of leaves, we have huge front-end loaders, all burning diesel fuel, which by the way, get about 4 miles to the gallon Mr. Ecologically Sound Practices. They run up and down the streets for weeks at a time in the fall, pushing our leaves around at a tremendous cost to the taxpayers, and spewing disgusting diesel exhaust all over our neighborhoods.

And while the huge loaders are pushing our leaves around burning diesel fuel at an ungodly rate, the big dump trucks lie in wait at strategic intersections, and next to them, another big tractor loader, just waiting, waiting and idling and burning more diesel fuel, waiting to load the leaves and spewing even more exhaust into the air. While all this leaf pushing around and engine idling is going on, and all this diesel fuel is being burned and all this exhaust is being blown into the air, well, I guess we're still getting rid of all those leaves, but there seems to be something missing, and something seems terrible wrong.

There're no neighbors talking anymore around the leaf piles, and there's no children playing anymore in the sunny, cool fall afternoons, and there's no time for chatting up your neighbors near the crackling of the burning piles of leaves, or the smell of smoke on your clothes when you finally went in for a cup of hot chocolate, or some cider, or a bowl of soup or chili. No, there's none of that going on anymore because someone had to protect us from ourselves and someone had to protect our precious atmosphere by substituting the diesel exhaust for the smoke from the burning leaves.

I don't know about you, but as I smelled that smell a couple of days ago and the childhood memories of fall and the images from those days long gone by came over me like a wave, I couldn't help but think that I'd gladly have a little more smoke in the air, maybe even a little more pollution, if I could just one more time, just once more, go outside and burn a pile of leaves without running afoul of the law. As my fishing partners and I like to say before we do something we know is stupid, "Hey, what's the worst that could happen?" I think I'm going to go burn a pile of leaves today; I'm just going to do it. What's the worst that could happen? And that is the "Loon Moment" for today.

From the "Loon Moment" – Nov. 26, 2006

Here's what I added two years later:

I've heard stories of authors taking ten years or more to finish their works. While I can't give you any specific examples, I'm sure you've heard similar tales. The lack of deadlines and the ability to take as long as you'd like with a book or story is a particularly appealing aspect of being an author, at least for me. In addition, the time lag between the starting and finishing points of some work, often allows for some new perspective to influence your original intentions. And so it is with this chapter of the book.

When I first broadcast "Memories of Burning Leaves", it was about nothing more than a wistful longing for days gone by, triggered by the wonderful smell of burning leaves on a fall day. The "I'm annoyed at government intrusion in our lives" part of the story was only a minor sub-theme. But as I write this postscript almost two and a half years later, and considering current events, nothing could loom larger in my mind than the seemingly unstoppable advance of our own government's intrusion into the most private and intimate parts of our lives.

A lot can happen in two and a half years. For those of you asleep at the switch, I'll give you a couple of highlights:

- *America has won the Iraq war. This still hasn't hit the major news networks yet, so I don't blame you if you missed this one.*
- *The entire financial system, which has been in place for the last half century or more, has completely collapsed. Believe it or not, I'm not sure most Americans truly comprehend the consequences of this truth yet.*
- *The country has elected its first African-American, socialist president. This is historic only because of the African-American thing. We've elected socialist presidents before.*
- *At the same time the country elected a socialist president, it also gave the socialist Democrat party control of both houses of the United States legislature.*
- *Appealing to our most basic fears to promote a left-wing socialist agenda, the president and congress are rapidly moving to pass legislation aimed at turning the country into*

another (take you pick France, England or Canada if you prefer).

- *At a <u>minimum</u>, the cost of this legislation will be to saddle our children and grandchildren, and perhaps even generations beyond our ability to count, with a crushing tax burden.*

- *In the <u>worst case</u>, it will trigger an economic downturn making the great depression seem like a picnic; fuel runaway inflation to match the Weimar Republic; create a health care system which gives the loving, caring Washington bureaucrats the power to decides who lives and who dies, and create a state where the government owns all, or at least a controlling interest, in the country's means of production (Auto industry, banks, etc..).*

As I write, it seems inevitable our congress will pass this or similar legislation; and I for one am scared to death by the prospects. Our founding fathers knew well, and specifically outlined in great detail for our benefit, the pitfalls, traps and conditions that could derail the "Grand Experiment" they so brilliantly constructed. The risk of losing our country is not some theoretical or academic exercise in a political science class. It is real and from my perch, it's happening as we speak.

*It's not too late though, "We the People" can still save our country and keep it from becoming another piece of rubbish thrown onto the trash heap of failed political experiments. Not only can we save our nation, it is our duty to do so. Thomas Jefferson wrote in the Declaration of Independence – " **But when a long train of abuses*** and usurpations, pursuing invariably the same Object evinces a design to reduce them under absolute Despotism, it is their right, it is their duty, to throw off such Government, and to provide new Guards for their future security."

Our future is at stake - right now. The very security and freedoms we've enjoyed since our founding are about to be lost for our children, grandchildren and great grandchildren. Lost is the wrong word, stolen is more accurate; stolen by a government out of control and out of touch with the people it is intended to serve. Our very nation, which has served as an example of freedom and righteousness to the entire world, is at risk of becoming unrecognizable to us. It is truly our right, and most certainly our sacred duty to change it before it's too late.

Scott Franz – February 2009

Ten
"Evy – The Wonder Dog"

It's that time again in the show for what we here at the Green Hour Show have come to affectionately call, the "Loon Moment". Now a lot of the "Loon Moments" have a message, or a lesson learned I like to share with you. I'm going to try hard to come up with one by the end this story, but to be honest; it's going to be a real stretch. I'll see what I can do.

Many years ago, back in the early years when my bride and I were still young and our children were still tots, we had two family dogs. One was a little Scottie named "Raisin", who I bought for my wife Ann on our first Christmas together. The other was a dog we acquired, or more precisely, rescued from an animal shelter, a year or two later, who we named Evy. Her formal name was "Evinrude" after the boat motor, because this dog was supposed to be the one that went fishing with me to keep me company. That never happened; she turned into a house dog almost instantly.

Now, one fall weekend, we drove down to central Illinois to visit my wife's parents and we packed up the whole family, dogs and all. I don't remember the occasion, but my wife's brothers were visiting that weekend as well, and we decided to go out to some farmland my farther-in-law owned to shoot some clay pigeons. He had about 80 acres located about 15 miles away from their family house.

At the last minute, as we were loading the guns and clay pigeons into the car, Ann thought it would be a good idea to take Evy out to the farm with us. I said sure and we hopped into the car, taking Evy with us, and headed out the fifteen miles to do some shooting.

When we first arrived and started getting set up to shoot, Evy seemed to be enjoying herself. She was a city dog, and I guess the smells and the freedom of running the fields were pretty new to her. She was having a great time, right up until the moment the first shotgun blast rang out, at which point she took off like a bat out of Hades.

At this point, I wasn't too worried. Even though I didn't see her, it was pretty open country and I figured she just go far enough away so that the shots didn't bother her and we'd find her easy enough when we were through shooting. After about an hour or so of shooting clay pigeons, we started to wrap things up and load the car. Right about that time, we started calling for the dog, but we got absolutely no response. She was nowhere to be found.

Ann's brothers and I spread out started walking the surrounding fields, calling for the dog and looking everywhere. We must have covered all eighty acres and another couple hundred to spare, at which point we started to get a little concerned. We were losing daylight fast, and it was going to be hard to spot an all black dog at night.

We decided to leave and then drove country roads to about five adjacent farms, looking as best we could in their fields from the road and knocking on every door to ask if anyone had spotted a dog and to please keep a lookout for it. It's not uncommon for lost dogs, once they get a little hungry, to head towards houses to see if they can scratch up a little food.

Well when we finally got back my in-laws house and told everyone we'd lost the dog, a general panic set in, and soon we were out searching again in the dark of night. This time there wasn't a farm house within a 10 mile radius we didn't stop at and talk to the owners, asking about the dog. Still, no dog showed up and at about 11:00 that night, we decided to resume the search in the morning.

I've always been an early riser, and so was Ann's dad. So at about 6:00 AM we got in his car and started to make the drive back up to the farm about 15 miles away. After we had driven about 10 miles, we spotted the dog on the side of the road. She'd been hit by a car and was dead. We picked her up and wrapped her in a blanket my father-in-law had in the trunk of the car and drove back to the house to break the bad news to Ann and the kids.

By the time we got there, everyone was up and we gave them the sad news. You can imagine how upset they were. Ann insisted we had to have a proper funeral for the dog, so with the kids all sobbing and crying uncontrollably, I dug a grave and solemnly laid poor Evy to rest. Ann and the kids painted a rock for a tombstone and the burial was complete, but the mourning had only just begun.

The rest of the day was just miserable. As soon as you thought they were coming around, the kids would just suddenly break into heartbreaking sobs and tears. The entire day went pretty much along those lines. There were a lot of people at the house for the weekend, so I had drawn a couch in the living room for a bed, and I when I was finally able to lay down to sleep for the night, I was thankful for the peace and I was hoping everyone's mood would improve a little by the next day.

I mentioned earlier that Ann's dad was an early riser, so about 6:00 AM the following morning, he was already up. He comes over to the couch I'm sleeping on, shakes me a little and when he sees I'm awake says, "Jack (that's a nickname I've always had), you've got to get up. You're not going to believe this." So I groggily get up, walked to the kitchen and there in the kitchen is Evy, all ragged, full of cockle-burs and mud and looking like she's been through hell.

Now when I saw my dog back from the dead and looked at my father-in-laws face, we started laughing like all hell at how stupid we had been to have picked up, held funeral services for and buried the wrong dog. I have no idea whose dog we buried, but I've got to tell you, that dog got a first-rate funeral complete with a headstone. I doubt its owners would have gone through as much trouble.

So we cleaned up "Evy the Wonder Dog" (her new name and well earned due to her amazing navigational abilities), fed her a good meal and she was all ready and presentable for when the rest of the family woke up. How that dog ever found its way back to a house she'd never been to before, from a farm she was driven to over fifteen miles away, I'll never know. But it sure made everyone happy that day and has given me a story to tell for all these years.

As I mentioned before, I like for each "Loon Moment" to have a purpose, or a lesson learned or some moral to the story. If there's one in this story, it's completely lost on me, but that won't keep me from telling this story to anyone who'll listen. You've got to admit, it's a doozie. And that is the "Loon Moment" for today.

From a "Loon Moment" – Never broadcast.

Some added comments about "Evy the Wonder Dog":

Many of the "Loon Moments" in this book are stories, which for me at least and after some reflection, speak to a larger life message or some life lesson I learned as a result. When I decided to revise "Loon Moments", I truly wanted to add a little something special to each of these stories or broadcasts, something which would clarify that message or lesson. After all, in the time-limited medium of radio, I wasn't always able to go as far as I wanted with each of my moments.

In telling this particular story, and after countless hours of reflection after the fact, I couldn't come up with a single thing that could even remotely be described as a life lesson. There's absolutely no instructional value, no uplifting moral and no deep message.

I've gotten a lot of mileage over the years telling this story, but I've never been sure what part of it amazes me most. While Evy's navigational skills in finder her way home from a strange place, such a long way from home was truly amazing, It paled in comparison to the amazing stupidity and utter ridiculousness of misidentifying and burying a strange dog.   How in the world can someone not recognize their own dog?

I guess in the end, the story simply shows how just about any moment you share with someone you care about, no matter how foolish, can be a "Loon Moment". For as long as I live, I will never forget the moment I locked eyes with my father-in-law and we shared the simultaneous realization we had carefully and reverently scraped an unknown dog from the roadway, and proceeded to provided a class A funeral- for someone else's dog. We've recounted it together several times over the years. To this very day, I laugh aloud.

Scott Franz – February 2009

Eleven
"Teach Your Children Well"

Now today's "Loon Moment" is about courage. Really, it's more about how badly misunderstood the word "courage" really is, particularly by the young men and women of this country.

The other night I woke up in the middle of the night with some ache or pain or something that disturbed my sleep. I think it was a shoulder, but it could have been any joint at my age, it really doesn't matter. So I got up and took a few aspirin and stretched back out on the couch in my living room. I instinctively turned on the television since I was now up and awake, and as the screen lights up and comes to life, the movie "Saving Private Ryan" is playing.

The movie is right at the part where the one, kind of wimpy, guy in the squad, who is the typist by trade I think, but who could speak German and so, against his will, gets put in the squad searching for Private Ryan. The scene is where he's cowering in fear in a hallway of a bombed out building during one of the final scenes, and he lets this German soldier, who's in a life and death struggle upstairs, kill one of the guys in his squad without lifting a finger to help. It appears he could have, and probably would have saved his life had he tried, but he was immobilized by fear.

The scene is very powerful because you could just feel this guy's absolute fear and terror, and at the same time, you could feel his absolute disgust and humiliation with himself for being such a coward, and for being so afraid and so terrified as to be absolutely incapable of action. If ever a guy was able to act and completely portray the internal and emotional tug of war this scene was supposed to depict, well this guy did it; it was absolutely great acting. He later redeems himself somewhat in the film, which brings up another point about courage I'll get to in a little while.

The scene I described in Saving Private Ryan really displayed the true essence of courage and the relationship courage has with fear. I think a lot of our youth today aren't taught about the real meaning of courage and specifically the special relationship and link fear has to courage. I truly believe courage is something we need to teach to our children. Let me explain.

We all know how to be afraid and don't need any coaching in that area; it's just pure instinct. We fear so many things as we go through life, many of them are justified and many are not. But the simple act of overcoming our fears IS an act of individual courage, no matter what those fears are or how justifiable they may be. Without fear there ABSOLUTELY CANNOT be any courage. The very definition of courage is the CONSCIOUS overcoming of fear. All unconscious acts that appear to be courageous, if they're born without fear, contain absolutely no aspects of courage to them at all. This is the message our children need to be taught. Very simply it's this; every moment of fear, every tinge or feeling of anxiety that causes us to pause, every instance of self-doubt which makes us afraid, and every single incident of societal temptation, is an opportunity; an opportunity to display our courage, or to act courageously and hence, to truly become courageous. What a great thing our fears truly become. Each and every one of them gives us the opportunity to CHOOSE to be courageous.

Here's the other thing that they need to be taught about courage and it's important; once a coward does not mean always a coward. I think kids aren't taught to understand this concept in the right way.

I've found a person only needs to prove to him or herself once that they have what it takes to be courageous; and from that point on, guess what, they truly are courageous; and they're no longer cowards. No matter how long they've previously been a coward, or no matter how many time they've previously succumbed to their fears, because ONE single act of courage by any one individual is truly a life changing act. In that one moment, he or she is instantly transformed from a coward into a brave man, or woman, or teenager, whatever age it happens. One time, that's all it takes.

This is a marvelous realization once a young man or woman experiences they have the courage to overcome their fears, or temptations or whatever they need to overcome with courage. What we as adults need to do is to encourage, well, courage. We need to constantly be preaching to our children and our young adults through every means possible, the need to live their lives LOOKING for opportunities to be courageous. We need to teach them they need to actively seek out what it is they fear; and when they discover what that is, to strive to overcome it.

But that's not what we do these days. As a society, we take our fears and instead of striving to overcome them, we now make excuses for them. We make excuses for our children, and our teenagers, and our young adults. Instead of challenging them to overcome these fears, we encourage them to give in to them, telling them it's not their fault. We group those with the same fears together, give it some fancy name, generally including the word "disorder", and make it a medical condition, One which can't be help and needs to be treated with medication.

I was reading once that George Patton was so afraid of being shot, specifically by a bullet aimed directly at the bridge of his nose; he purposely stood up in the line of fire at a shooting range to overcome his fear. While that's a little extreme, it's symbolically at least, exactly what needs to be done with fear in order to eliminate it. In order to develop the courage we need in life and to live courageously, we need to confront our fears.

So anyway, this scene from "Saving Private Ryan" got me thinking about courage, and the lack of it we seem to have in society today, and our overall failure as a society to teach the importance and meaning of courage to our youth. I was starting to get all bummed out about it and I actually started to FEAR for the future of our country because of it. Interestingly enough, just at that moment, even though it was late at night, I walked into my home office and sat down at my computer. On it was an e-mail from a friend of mine who had forwarded a bunch of pictures of our troops in Iraq.

The pictures, and there were lots of them, brought me back and gave me hope. They were pictures of very young men and women, all in very dangerous situations, displaying unspeakable courage. Not mindless acts of bravado, not at all. You could actually see the fear and the animal-like caution in their eyes from the pictures. Yet as scared as they most probably were, they showed our boys and girls performing their duties with a steady determination and grit in spite of their obvious fear. As I looked at these pictures, I no longer feared for the future of our country. I knew, right then and there, we still have enough sons and daughters with parents who taught them about courage, as well as duty and honor.

So as we start our celebrations during this Christmas season, afraid we won't be able to get that play station before the stores run out. Or as we go about our holiday chores without a care in the world, except whether or not we'll get all our shopping done on time, we should probably stop and think about all those brave young men and women who are overcoming their fears every single day. They're doing their duty with a steadiness and determination not even they thought they would ever be capable of, yet they somehow manage. And they manage it with courage; the courage Americans have displayed through so many generations and so many wars and so many thousands of gallons of blood. At that very moment I was so proud of them, and so proud of their parents and finally, so proud to be an American.

So whenever you get a little disgusted with what you see in our politics these days, or in our schools, or in our courts, just think and reflect for a moment about those young men and women serving in our military and everything will make sense again and seem OK. And that is the "Loon Moment" for today.

From the "Loon Moment" Dec. 2, 2006

I wish I would have added this:

As I examine my life from time to time, I find I have few, if any regrets. I guess that surprises even me as I reflect on what some would describe as a somewhat tumultuous life. The one which comes to mind rather constantly though is the fact I never served in the military. It wasn't really my fault I didn't serve, although I guess I could have always enlisted after the draft ended. Viet Nam wound down without my ever being called; and by the time I was eligible, the winding down was accelerating pretty quickly as our leaders struggled to find a way out.

During the course of that war, there was no such thing as war protesters and draft dodgers where I grew up. Our neighborhood had gold and blue stars hanging from more windows than I could count, and I went to enough funerals to last me for quite some time. Mostly, they were the not-so-much older brothers of the kids I grew up with. I remember the pain and the anguish of the families and their friends. I remember the flag-draped caskets. I remember the lonely one or two uniformed representatives of the armed forces present at those funerals and I remember the solemn looks on their faces. There were no twenty-one gun salutes and no military parades; Just the simple presentation of a folded flag. I also remember that in spite of the grief, there was also a quiet pride for the fallen. They were called, they went, and they paid the ultimate price. In return, they were honored with the pride and respect of their families and communities. At least that's how it played out in my community.

In a very weird way, I was always a little jealous of the fallen back them and I guess I'm a little jealous of our young men and women serving today. My jealousy is likely the root of my regret for not serving; and my jealousy is surely born of this one simple fact: those who've served are better than me, and I know it. It's a little hard to admit but it's true. I feel small and selfish in comparison to those who've served our country so selflessly, and rightly so. I feel like a scavenger, feasting off the bounty of freedom and safety they've provided without contributing at all to the feast. How could one not feel small in comparison?

Well at least I can admit it's my jealousy. The left in this country is jealous of our military too, but they can't admit it. It's hard for them to digest the fact that bright, young, patriotic men and woman want to serve their country. They mask their feelings of inferiority by being disrespectful to those in uniform; and they demean the military every chance they get. We see it every day. They try to get the ROTC thrown off college campuses. They insinuate the military's for the poor and underprivileged alone; the best chance for the dimmest and dullest among us; not a real option for bright, intelligent young men and women.

The generation that answered the call for World War II is sometimes called the "greatest generation", and there's no doubt they did a great thing against tremendous odds. But they had the country behind them every step of the way, and they were showered with honor, respect and parades upon their return from war. They returned to a booming post war economy, jobs and the GI bill.

I don't mean at all to diminish the contributions or sacrifices of that generation, but I don't know how you can look at the young men and women in our military today and not be filled with pride, joy and hope for our future. They are truly the best among us.

Hopefully we still have a whole lot of history yet to write as a nation. I don't know for sure, but with everything that's happening in the world today, I get the feeling our military will play a big part in how that history gets written. Perhaps we should reserve labeling any one generation of those who serve as "the greatest". Personally, I think they're all great and I thank God for them every single day.

Scott Franz – November 2008

Twelve
"Your Children Listen"

As you know by now, I reserve this segment of the show every week for the "Loon Moment". Can I have a little mood music please maestro? Thank you. There's nothing like the call of a loon to set the mood. If you're listening for the first time, the "Loon Moment" is a segment in our show which often can be a little reflective, and sometimes it's a moment we can share with each other about our experiences in nature, either those awe inspiring, or frightening, or just plain weird moments. But today's "Loon Moment" is simply a cry for help. I'm serious now. It's a cry for help from me, directly to you. It's only loosely related to nature as it has to do with my new hunting dog "Buckshot". Well he's not exactly new. He's about a year old now and I'm pulling my hair out over this dog. So if you have any clue as to how to train a Labrador Retriever, please call me at the show today and help me out, because I'm truly about to lose my mind.

Now, I don't know if I've ever told you the story of how I ended up with this dog or not. He's a golden Labrador retriever named "Buckshot"; with green eyes. He's really a very good natured animal, BUT, he's a complete maniac; and I really need some help. I swear to you there's absolutely nothing this dog won't eat or chew on, and that's where I need your help. I don't know if this is a Labrador trait or if I just have a weird dog, but I'm not kidding, you can't turn you back on this dog for a second and he's eating something he shouldn't. He also seems to have a special liking for plants and wood of any kind. I mean, he rips off huge branches from my shrubs, or he'll break off low hanging branches from trees. He digs up the roots of anything and eats them, I swear don't know what to do with this dog.

Anyway here's the deal on how I ended up with 'ol Buckshot. Last Thanksgiving, my wife and kids and I went, as we usually do, down to my in-laws for the Thanksgiving holiday. Actually it's only my father-in-law now, as my mother in law passed away several years ago.

He lives in central Illinois, where he's lived all his life, right in the heart of farm country. If you're unfamiliar with small town America, everyone knows everyone and any major event, like the birth of a litter of dogs, or gaggle of new baby lambs (do sheep have gaggles of lambs or is it herds? Being a city kid, I'm not really sure) is generally known by everyone in town. A common activity is to take the smaller kids to go see whatever species having cute babies. Anyway, this Thanksgiving, my father-in-law's secretary had a dog, which just gave birth to a new litter of chocolate Labrador retrievers. Per the small town rules, my father-in-law decided to take all the grandchildren out to see the puppies at her farm (everyone lives on a farm no matter what their _real_ occupation is). I decided to go along and drive some of the kids for him.

Before we all left, I just happened to mention, **out loud** to my wife, that if they were good looking dogs, I might just take one of them as I'd been thinking about getting a hunting dog. Our family border collie of many years "Cesar" was getting on in years; was getting very, very arthritic and even though I didn't think he was anywhere close to the end of his days, I also didn't think he was going to live for too many more years. I thought it might be a good idea to get a transitional dog. It just always seemed to me to be a lot easier to train a new puppy if he's got a great example around to show him the ropes. So after mentioning I might pick one out, I immediately got "THE LOOK" from my bride of 27 years and a stern, "don't you dare bring a dog home". By the way, she's always said this to me right before I've gone out to bring home any family dog we've ever had.

So we went out to look at the dogs, and they REALLY were great looking labs. I thought one might just serve the dual purpose of both getting the family a transitional dog and also a great future bird dog for me. Unfortunately, they weren't quite ready to leave their momma yet or I probably would have left the farm with a new chocolate Labrador.

When we all got back to the house right before the Thanksgiving feast began, I announced to my wife, and to everyone else within earshot, I was going to call the dog's owner later that week and reserve one of the puppies for my new bird dog. I'd come back as soon as they were weaned and pick him or her up. At that point, my bride threw a somewhat standard, but an admittedly pretty low-keyed "we don't need another dog" fit. She claimed first, I was too busy to train a new dog, second, she didn't want another dog, and finally, if we got another dog, she was going to end up taking care of it and training it and so on. This was a standard protest, all of which she absolutely knew I would ignore if I really wanted the dog because I also knew three things about my bride:

- One, I knew she's a bigger sucker for dogs than I am.
- Two, it takes her all of about ten minutes to fall in love with any dog and she can only keep up the act that she's mad about it for about a half a day - tops, and long before the half-day is through, she'd be holding and petting the dog at the same time she'd be snarling at me for procuring it.
- Three, a half-day of your wife being mad at you is absolutely nothing to weather for a guy who's been married for 27 years, especially if you end up with a great new bird dog in the deal.

So anyway, I put up a short 30 second, fake fight for a few minutes on behalf of men everywhere and then dropped the whole subject and had a nice Thanksgiving dinner.

Now here's the thing, and the big difference between men in their 40's and 50's, as opposed to men in their 20's and 30's. Men my age still talk about doing things impulsively, and occasionally we do them. After all, we are still men. But more often now, we actually **think** about things for a day or two before doing them, and often we come to the conclusion that what seemed like a great idea at the time, is probably not so great an idea after all. Now we still run about 50-50 on doing stupid things like buying new dogs, or new boats and other stupid things of that nature; things which we generally want but don't have enough time to use, and absolutely insist we're going to find the time for and do more often anyway. In this case though, the bottom line was that after a day, I knew my wife was right. I was way too busy to train a new dog and it wasn't fair to just drop one on her. So I just forgot about it and never said another word about it – to anyone.

I've noticed a phenomenon with children, and it doesn't matter how old they get. Fathers need to be very careful what we say around them. I think this applies only to fathers, I'm not really sure, and I haven't exactly conducted a scientific study. But the phenomena is this: Whatever comes out of your mouth, whether you're just throwing out ideas, using the people around you for sounding boards, or if your just talking garbage for the fun of it, Your Children Believe What You Say and take it the gospel's truth. Now for someone like me, who tends to like to verbalize ideas and things I'm only just considering, bad ideas along with the good, this tendency becomes problematic from time to time. This was one of those times.

I had completely discarded and forgotten the idea of getting another dog by the day after Thanksgiving. That didn't stop my children from believing the single most important thing missing from my life was a new hunting dog. So a couple days before Christmas, I came into the office and my son met me at the door asking me if I wanted an early Christmas present. Of course, I said yes and he leads me into his office. There sits a puppy named "Buckshot", a beautiful little golden Labrador with green eyes.

While trying to not ruin his surprise, I tried to break it to him gently that he'd just thrown me under a fast moving bus and buried me with his mother, my wife. She would never believe, not in a million years, that I wasn't somehow a part of a conspiracy to bring a new dog into the house.

When I gently broke the news to my bride, this time it was not a low-keyed fit. It was the real thing, a full blown storm and a real nor'easter at that. It took me a good day to convince her that I had nothing to do with this and that our son had taken it upon himself to bring this dog into our lives.

Now fortunately, after a day she was in love with the new puppy, like I knew she would be, and it seemed that everything would be OK. But things had just begun to get interesting.

Apparently, my son bought Buck from one of those puppy mills stores, that isn't exactly known for their humane treatment of animals or responsible business practices. It turns out old Buckshot hadn't had all of its shots, was sick as a dog (no pun intended) and was contagious to boot. All of this was unbeknownst to my son. Within a day or two of bringing Buckshot home, both he and my faithful border collie Cesar were raging sick; both of them coughing and hacking with some sort of kennel cough disease and some other unknown viral infection. The kind of illnesses you generally don't bring home with a dog if you're dealing with reputable dog breeders.

So within days the visits to the vets start and Buckshot being a strong, young dog recovers rather quickly. Cesar, on the other hand does not, and he goes through a series of ups and downs that manage to keep him going to the vet about once a day for the next three weeks; all the time racking up doctor bills that would make a world class heart surgeon blush. I've got a theory about veterinarians, used-car salesman and dentists, I'll share it with you later (and of course, this would not apply to any vet, used-car salesman or dentist with the kind of character required to read this book). The bottom line is this: after about three weeks, my dog of ten years has passed away, my new puppy Buckshot, my son and I are all equally blamed and vilified for a month for being "dog-killers", as well as idiots, and poor Buckshot can hardly get anyone in the family to look at him, much less pet him for a good month, except for me. The poor dog was being punished because he had been the unwitting instrument of death to our beloved family dog Cesar.

Now to prove my point about veterinarians, used car salesman and dentists all being in the same boat, after Cesar died, my wife calls the vet's to see about disposing of the body (this was before I could get back from the office after he passed away to talk some sense into her) and believe it or not, they wanted to do an autopsy to determine the cause of death. I almost hit the ceiling. Were they really saying, really admitting, they didn't know what in the heck they were treating the dog for to the tune of about $6,000 now that he was dead? I mean if they needed to do an autopsy to figure it out now, it means they either didn't know, or WORSE, they were trying to take further advantage of a very upset woman who had just lost a dear pet. One who'd stayed up with a sick dog for the past several weeks like she would with a sick child. I don't know and I'll let you draw your own conclusions.

There're a few points to today's story, some more important than others. First, I wanted to introduce you to my new dog, Buck. I know you'll be hearing more about him in future "Loon Moments", so I had to introduce him to you at some point.

Second, watch out for veterinarians. I'm sure there are some great one's out there, but there's a lot of rotten ones as well. They know you're emotionally invested in the animals you bring to them and some of them will suggest the most intricate surgeries and procedures, knowing you don't want to lose your pet. As much as you love your dog or cat, or other family pet, I've never seen one worth the cost of a heart transplant. Try and stay a little grounded.

Now the real moral of today's story is this: be very careful what you say around your children. I swear to GOD they're listening, even if you don't think they are. Every single word you say to them is important. Even when they fight, resist, or you think they're not, trust me, they're listening. Make it count. And that is the "Loon Moment" for today.

From the "Loon Moment" – Oct. 21, 2006

Here's what I would have liked to have added:

Parenting and raising children is hard enough as it is without having to watch every word you utter. If we realized just how closely our children really listen to us, it would probably scare you into being a mute. Like it or not though, they do listen; and the fact they do, simply heaps another awesome responsibility onto our already burdened shoulders as parents.

If you need any further pressure as a parent, I've got more good news for you. In addition to listening, they're watching. They're watching everything you do and not only that, they're comparing what you say against what you do. It's enough to make you want to stay in bed until they hit the age of thirty.

For those of you who fear the myriad of outside influences your children are exposed to as they morph from stage to stage, fear not. YOU are still the single most important influence in your child's life. If that didn't sink in the first time, let me say it again. YOU are the single most important influence on your child's life. Trust me on this one; I know it to be true.

So you'd better be consistent, you'd better tell them the truth, and above all, keep your promises to them, and make them keep theirs to you. Your children listen. Make it count.

Scott Franz – December 2007

Thirteen
"Thank God for Dads"

Here we are again. It's time for the "Loon Moment" segment of our show. I really love this segment of the show. I guess I've kind of been taking the first segment, or the first hour of the show and I've been using it to get out all my frustrations with politics and the rest of the crazed things that happen in the world. But by this time in the show, I've got to get centered again. I've been able to talk to you a little bit, talk myself down a little bit, and well by now I'm relaxed, I'm calm, and I'm ready for the peace, serenity and the tranquility of the "Loon Moment".

For those of you who are new to the show and new to this hour (because it hasn't really been that long since the "Green Hour" has become essentially the "Green Two Hours"), the "Loon Moment" is the part of the show where you and I can share either a great memory of the outdoors with each other, or a moment where we've been inspired or awed by nature, or even frightened by its power. It can also be something humorous about some time spent out in nature. But in the final analysis, whatever it's about, The "Loon Moment" should always leave you with a little something more - you know what I mean. It should either contain a lesson learned from that moment in nature, or maybe something, just a little something special you've taken from that moment you'll keep with you for a long time - maybe even for the rest of your life. It's one of those moments I want to share with you today. In actuality, it's really more of a summary of a lot of those moments.

Now we're rapidly approaching Thanksgiving. I guess this is actually the show before the Thanksgiving holiday, and as we contemplate a bit about the things we're thankful for, one of the things I always end up being thankful for is my DAD. In today's world dads, as a group that is, have been pretty marginalized. Let's face it, one of the primary goals of the feminist movement over the years has been to de-emphasize the role of men, and dads in the family unit. They claim there's no need for men anymore. Children don't need two parents, and all men bring to the table are a bunch of barbaric tendencies all children would be better off without. Like it or not, that's been their message for years now. I'm here to tell you not to believe it for a second.

I talk a lot about the outdoors. I talk about my fishing trips, hunting trips, backpacking trips and my survival skills. I've acquired the ability to talk about these things after years of being an outdoorsman. If I do say so myself, I'm a pretty skilled outdoorsman and feel as comfortable sleeping out under the open sky as I do sleeping in my own bed. In fact, I'm probably more comfortable outside because my bed really stinks. My wife and I paid a fortune for that thing and it's like sleeping on a rock. I digress. As I was saying, I'm a pretty skilled outdoorsman from all the time I've spent outdoors, but the funny part is, I have no idea who specifically taught me all those skills. I mean, I was a boy scout and all, and my Dad started taking me fishing way up north probably when I was around

10 or 11 years old. But I can't remember anyone ever teaching me all the things I know about hunting and fishing and survival skills. The one person I'm <u>absolutely</u> sure didn't teach me those things, was my father. Fortunately he doesn't listen to the show, so I'm not going to get in trouble when I tell you, as outdoorsmen go, he is by far the worst I've ever seen. This would really kill him to hear because he loves fishing and appreciates nature so much, but he's just a terrible fisherman and outdoorsman. I'm Sorry Dad.

I started off this moment by telling you as we get closer to Thanksgiving, one of the things I'm most grateful for, most thankful for is my Dad. Obviously after I just got done trashing him as an outdoorsman, I'm obviously not grateful for his teaching me about those outdoor kind of things. But even though he was never very good at any of those things himself, and even though he could never teach me those things, some of the best moments I've ever spent in my life were spent in the outdoors with my DAD, mostly spent fishing. During those times, he gave me a most marvelous gift. He exposed me to the grandeur and the beauty of the outdoors.

One of the things that always strikes me the most upon reflection, and I think it struck me first when I was in my teen years (if you can remember back then just how charming you we're to your parents during those years), was that all of the angst for <u>both</u> of us would go away during the time we spent together fishing. No matter what we had been fighting or grousing at each other about up until then, it all went away. It seemed we would talk about things in a different way during those times, and we'd talk about things we generally never talked about.   Maybe it was because, during those years, I never really realized my parents had stresses, concerns and troubles as well. I guess all those stresses would melt away for my Dad, as well as for me during the times we spent fishing. There we'd both be, appreciating the same things, mostly the beauty and tranquility of the country, the fantastic sunsets, the clean air, and it seemed to just open up doors we just couldn't get opened anywhere else. We'd talk; we'd talk about the world, man to man now, even though I wasn't really qualified as one yet. I found out how confusing life could get for him sometimes, as well as for me. What I ended up getting out of it most out of our time together were the rules: The "Rules for Men". It was laid out for me how real men were to behave in this world, regardless of how they felt, or what was happening to them or around them, or because of them. No matter what, there were the rules; Rules for Behaving like a Man.

Now I hate to pick on the feminist movement. That can get you in a lot of trouble these days.   But the one thing they never understood, still do not understand, and will probably never understand, is that only men can raise other men. Only men can teach young boys "The Rules", and show them how to act and behave as men. I'm talking about real men now, not the sissified, crying, touchy, feely, Oprah Win-Free-Eyed kind of men. Not the kind of men the feminists want us to be (at least till they need a real man), but real men. The kind of men who get up day after day, no matter how they feel, and provide for their families.   The kind of men who know the rules and live by them, day in and day out. Not the kind of men who need to explore their feelings, or the kind who need to find themselves. No, I'm talking about the kind of men who have no need of doing any of those things. There's no need, because all they need are "The Rules" of men as taught to them by other men.

Now you may be asking yourself, what are these rules I'm talking about?? I'm not going to go over them today, mostly because every real man out there knows what I'm talking about, and 99% of you learned what I'm talking about from your DAD.

I don't think it's any real mystery why we have so many societal problems today. I directly link them to the marginalization of men and their importance to the family over the past decades. Don't get me wrong, without mothers we'd be in trouble as well. They're natural nurturers and our children desperately need that in those early years and often times well beyond. Can anyone comfort like a mother? No way.

But make absolutely no mistake about it, without a man in the family, without someone who can be a rock, steady and strong for their family regardless of what is happening all around him, or to him or even because of him; without someone steady and strong to protect you, someone you absolutely know will not let anything bad happen to you, and who would lay down his life in defense of you, well, without that, families are in trouble. No one can fill that role like a strong dad.

Strong dads are a huge brake constantly being applied to bad behavior within a family. How many of you grew up getting sassy a little early in life with your mother, but wouldn't dare try that out on DAD. Where in the world do you think the phrase," Wait until your father gets home" comes from? It comes from a time when fathers were respected and were the disciplinarians within a family. They were awesomely good at being disciplinarians too, all without ever saying a word. A look from dad was usually good enough to stop any unwanted behavior in its tracks.

But those times are gone and we're told fathers aren't needed anymore. Two men can raise children as well as a mother and a father, or two women, or two whatever. There's <u>No</u> need for Dad, or so they tell us. There's no need for his old fashioned rules, no need for his steadiness in times of crisis. We don't need dads; we just need more therapists…Right? Personally the best therapy I ever got was the time I spent, and the times I still spend with my Dad.

So Dad, if you're listening, I don't care that you're a rotten fisherman. I don't care that you can't field-dress a deer and I don't care you've never even handled a gun, much less fired one. But thanks for teaching me "The Rules". And don't worry, I didn't forget. I passed on "The Rules" to my son. It looks like they've stuck and he's going to be OK as well. And that is the "Loon Moment" for today.

From the "Loon Moment" – Nov. 18, 2006

Here's my later addition:

It's been several years since I broadcast this moment on the radio. Since then my father's health has deteriorated a little more, he's gotten a little more deaf and a little more forgetful. But then again, so have I.

I don't know how much longer I'll have him before he steps off the bus (that's his terminology, not mine, lest you find me too callous). I hope for a very long time. While neither of us knows for sure, we both assume he'll step off that bus before I do. I try not to think about it too much. I can't bear the thought of being fatherless, no matter how old I get. If the very thought is unimaginable and painful to me, a man over fifty with my own grown children, try and imagine how it feels for all the fatherless children in this world. I can; and it hurts just thinking about it.

The circumstances really don't matter. Whether they're fatherless by virtue of a death, divorce, or abandonment, the bottom line is they're still fatherless; and because they are, in some unavoidable and deep way – it hurts. They'll always have a void that can't be filled, and there's no substitute or replacement. In case any of you were wondering, two mommies do not make a daddy or equal a missing father, I don't care how many sociological studies you fudge. Even worse, two fathers are not better than one. The very thought gives me the shivers – talk about confusing a young male.

I'm sorry to tell the feminists, the social engineers, the gay-lesbian-transgendered activists, the atheist secularists and any other group who've set out to destroy the family unit to advance their own agendas, but fathers are <u>equally</u> one-half of something very, very *important; and they can't be replaced or substituted for, no matter how much BS science is used.*

I could go on forever about this topic, but you get the point. I know real men aren't perfect, but they are necessary. I know most women don't appreciate us simplistic Neanderthals fortunate enough to be raised by real men, until they need one. It doesn't bother me. But I worry a lot about a country that's marginalized fathers and men for so long. I worry about the new breed of men it will produce; men who really don't know how to be men. How could they if they've never been taught?

My dad and I don't fish together anymore; he's not as stable as he once was and he can't get in and out of the boat anymore. But when we're alone and get a chance to talk, we still talk about things the same way I described on those early fishing trips. We talk about the world, man to man, as equals. In many ways it's a little different now, we're both in different places and we've each racked up a whole lot more experience. We don't have the tranquil settings anymore of a northern lake, or of the setting sun over the jack pines, but in all of the important ways, it's still the same. After each and every one of these talks, I always have the same thought – Thank God for Dads.

Scott Franz – December 2008

Fourteen
"The Dribble Gene"

It is now time for that segment of our show, which I affectionately call the "Loon Moment". As you are by now well aware, the "Loon Moment" is the segment in our show where I like to share with you some of my experiences in, with, and about nature and the outdoors. At the end most "Loon Moments", I often try to impart to you, if there are any, the lessons I've learned from those experiences.

I've been informed, as the host of the "Green Hour", I must disclose to you the fact that although a deep, philosophical, sentimental, personally moving, motivating or deeply religious message is very often the intended result of many "Loon Moments", not all "Loon Moments" contain, nor does the host of this show warrant, imply or guarantee in any way, shape or form a deep, philosophical, sentimental, personally moving, motivating or deeply religious experience to any single listener, and that any listener experiencing such a moment as I just described by virtue of listening to the aforementioned "Loon Moment", does so strictly of their own accord and agrees to hold the host of the "Loon Moment" harmless. That being said, we can move on.

I'm probably dating myself when I talk about or mention the old Sears catalogs, but I'm sure many of you will remember them and can also remember, as I do, just how much fun it was to read and how much their arrival was anticipated.

Sears doesn't make a master catalog anymore, or if they do, they don't send it out to every household in America like they once did. I guess it's just too expensive. And Sears isn't the retailer it was way back then. But back in the day, you could get anything at Sears, and they **were** the nation's retailer. You could find anything and everything in the Sears Catalog; and there was something of interest for everyone. Children would build their Christmas lists and dreams as they poured page by page through the toy section of the catalog. Dad could find everything from guns, to tools, to furnaces. You name it, and the Sears Catalog had it.

So none of us have the Sears master catalog to look forward to anymore, and we haven't for quite some time. But for those of us who truly enjoy getting lost for an hour or two each year when the catalog came out, studiously reading the description of each and every item: Fear not. The experience is not lost. Not only is the experience not lost, it's been replaced; and for me at least, with one every bit as good, and in some ways far better. This new experience allows me to exercise an ability and personality trait we all probably need to work on a bit; the ability to FOCUS. And, you can find that kind of focus in, a little drum roll please, the Bass Pro Shops "Fishing Master Catalog".

To someone like me, the "Fishing Master Catalog" fulfills, in much the very same way the old Sears catalogs did, but with the added laser-like focus on fishing, and on everything you'd ever need or want to go fishing. You can find everything in the "Fishing Master

Catalog". From boats, and motors, to everything you could ever think of to outfit your boat.

For fishing gear, it's a regular cornucopia. The "Master Catalog" has everything from fishing rods, to reels, to lures, to tackle and tools and, well basically anything and everything you'd ever need to find, catch, keep, process and eat - a fish. All of this can be found in the "Fishing Master Catalog". And not only can you find everything you need, but there's choice, lots of choices. Every manufacturer is represented, and every type and size and color of lure can be found. Now this is what I call - focus. The focus and attention to detail of this catalog trickles right down to the tiniest of hooks and weights, to the most obscure jig, swivel or plastic worm. This catalog demonstrates to me, the very <u>essence</u> of focus.

Yes, the "Fishing Master Catalog" has it all, and when the glorious day arrives, the day when the "Fishing Master Catalog" is delivered right to your door, well now, it's not only a day you receive the most focused book on the planet, but it's a day for you to focus personally as well. And that is really the point of today's "Loon Moment" - Focus.

I might be wrong, but it seems to me a lot of people seem to lack focus these days. Not just a lack focus when it comes to the larger issues in life, but in the simple, day to day, moment to moment things as well. In fact, it seems to me, an awful lot of people are just simply oblivious to things going on or happening immediately around them. It's no wonder it's hard for them to focus on bigger things.

I know you know what I'm talking about. Just take a look around you and you'll see what I mean. Men are reading newspapers and books, or women are putting make-up on as they drive. Did you hear me? As they drive cars. They'd like you to believe they're multi-tasking. They're not; it's simply a lack of focus; not to mention a little stupidity.

One thing I often do to test people's focus is to put my hand out for my change immediately after I give a bill to a cashier. I can't tell you how many times my change gets dropped on the counter, a good foot away from my hand, by the usually uninterested and most definitely unfocused clerk. They somehow expect me to get my hand under where they drop the coins as they talk on the phone, or look out the window, or focus on anything else except giving me my change. I know being a clerk may not exactly be a dream job for some people, and I understand they may view it as only temporary, or perhaps even beneath them, but for God's sake, if you chose to take a job as a clerk – then focus a little and do your job.

I'm not claiming to exactly be a "Jedi Knight" myself, with lightening reflexes, but I am aware of things going on around me. I watch where I step, I rarely bump into things and I never get stuff I'm wearing caught on door knobs. What I'm saying is I try, and I try very hard to focus on what I'm doing, right at the minute I'm doing it. It seems like a simple thing to do, but amazingly a lot of people have trouble. They're way too busy mentally, to stay in the moment long enough to focus on what they're doing.   ,

I will admit I seem to have one problem when it comes to focus, but in my defense, I'm not really sure if it's a problem with my focus or a genetic defect. I'm leaning towards, and I'm pretty sure I've settled on genetic defect. To my dismay, it seems I've inherited the "dribble gene".

The "dribble gene" is a genetic defect that makes it absolutely impossible to get food or drink into your mouth without spilling some of it on your shirt. The reason I think its genetic is because my father has it, I have it and it seems I've passed it on to all of my children. It's very much like The Force from "Star Wars". From what I understand, the "dribble gene" is supposed to be a recessive and a very undesirable gene; and the only people who truly appreciate it are dry cleaners and shirt makers.

In our family line, the "dribble gene" now appears to have achieved a certain amount of dominance, and while still undesirable, it's at least become manageable. All of us inflicted carry those little spot remover sticks; much in the same way as people who are allergic to bees carry the "Epi-pen". With both, one truly focused shot takes care of everything.

Now focus is a marvelous tool when employed properly, and with it you can accomplish fantastic things. It takes a while, but you can actually improve your ability to focus with practice. If you've been able to stick with me through this loon moment and can now see and make the connection between my original legal disclaimer, the "Sears" catalog, the "Fishing Master Catalog" and the "dribble gene", you have achieved a highly advanced ability to intensely focus. If you weren't, you need more practice, and well, focus. And that is the "Loon Moment" for today.

From the "Loon Moment" – January 13, 2007

Added after the passage of the Economic Recovery and Reinvestment Act of 2009:

Obviously, not all "Loon Moments" were written after thoughtful reflection on some important value or moral principle. If a deep philosophical thought process was a prerequisite for every" Loon Moment" I ever broadcast, the hissing, crackling static of "dead air" would have been a common occurrence. The moment above is a testament to that fact.

As I add this postscript though, current events have managed to supply a more "focused" point to this otherwise rambling "moment". Last night, our elected representatives in congress passed the "Economic Recovery and Reinvestment Act of 2009", a monstrous 800 billion, 1000 page plus, spending bill. It was voted on in the dead of night, without a single representative having an opportunity to actually read its contents. There's some focus for you, eh? For the several weeks preceding its passage, it was being sold to the American public by the president and the democrat controlled congress as an urgently needed stimulus package. In the words of our new President, passage of this bill is needed to prevent a "Crisis from becoming a Catastrophe".

The debate on whether direct government spending actually stimulates the economy is something I can neither argue nor resolve in a few paragraphs, so I'll leave it for another time. What I can say is this: IF government spending has any chance at all of stimulating the economy, it must be FOCUSED and targeted at specific objectives. It has to focus on and target it's spending on projects designed to create jobs over the long-term. So you be the judge; how focused and targeted do you think these worthwhile projects are?

- *Filipino veterans, most of whom do not live in the United States, will get $200 million in long-awaited compensation for service in World War II.*
  - **Weren't they paid already? I think we should be able to find the cancelled checks somewhere.**
- *The deal provides $8 billion for high-speed rail projects, for example, including money that could benefit a controversial proposal for a magnetic-levitation rail line between Disneyland, in California, and Las Vegas, a project favored by Harry Reid. The 311-mph train could make the trip from Sin City to TomorrowLand in less than two hours, according to backers.*
  - ***I'd like to levitate Harry Reid right back to Arizona.***
- *Another $800 million is set aside for other carbon-capture projects, and a clause allows the money to go to projects that use petroleum coke instead of coal. This would probably benefit a company called Hydrogen Energy, which is jointly*

owned by British Petroleum and the multinational mining company Rio Tinto.

- o **British Petroleum and Rio Tinto. Two good 'ol American companies.**
- *The Senate version of the bill did not name a recipient but would have provided $2 billion for "one or more near zero emissions power plant(s)." The provision was clearly directed at reviving the FutureGen Alliance project, a proposed "clean coal" plant in Illinois.*
  - o **If we haven't yet learned by now, anything having to do with Illinois should be immediately suspect.**

Oops, I forgot to mention the 35 million targeted to save the San Francisco Salt Marsh mouse from extinction; that's a lot of mouse feed.

In addition to not being able to focus on the actual details of the largest spending bill in the history of our nation; that would have required their being able to actually read it prior to voting, our guys had a really tough time keeping their focus on spending and stimulus alone as they drafted this nifty bit of legislation. As Nancy Pelosi drove this bill to passage in record time, she and her colleagues drifted over into the atheist, leftist, secular agenda lane of traffic.

Thanks to this stimulus plan, it is now law that the even the word "prayer" cannot be mentioned in a school or classroom that receives any stimulus money for renovating their facilities. The bill also:

- *Lays the groundwork for nationalizing our healthcare system and establishes a "National Health Care Rationing Board". Think about this for a moment.*
- *Rolls back Welfare reform.*
- *Establishes dangerous protectionism.*
- *Funds unnamed renewable energy and other "Green" initiatives.*

I could go on, but you get the point. The stimulus bill, which in a few short days will become law, is a socialist's dream come true. It is either the culmination of, or lays the future groundwork, for every single leftist, socialist, atheist, secularist agenda ever dreamed up.

Oops once again. Maybe the commies in congress were a lot more focused than I thought.

Scott Franz – February 14, 2009

Fifteen
"A Loon Moment Christmas"

It's time again in our show for what we have now come to affectionately call "The Loon Moment". I've got to tell you, I'm really feeling the pressure to deliver a superb "Loon Moment" today. I mean with this being the Christmas show and everything, I'm really feeling the heat. In retrospect, I guess I've been warming up to it for a while, as I've tended to take something of a religious bent during this segment in recent weeks. And I suppose if ever there was a time to tie the "Loon Moment" into some deeper, moral lesson, I guess the show right before the holiday celebrating the birth of Christ would be a good one to do it on. So I'm feeling a little pressure today and I'm going to try my best.

I have a forest preserve pretty close to my house and I often walk along the trails there with my dog "Buckshot". For being just a little patch of woods in an urban area, it's an amazingly quiet and tranquil place. There's a trail that runs along a nice little river which runs a good mile, maybe more, and I rarely see anyone as I walk. So I generally let "Buckshot" run ahead of me, and I'll find some good sticks I'll toss for him to fetch (which he absolutely loves). I generally take a good walking stick myself. There's just something about a good walking stick and a good piece of wood in your hands.

Anyway, I've become very familiar with these woods and well I should, because I grew up around them and actually spent a lot of time playing in them as a kid. We'd build dams across the river and make forts, all the things little boys do in the woods when they're 8 or 10 years old, which, by the way, it seems they can't do anymore for fear of running into Mr. Stranger Danger, but that's beside the point. For a small patch of woods that been land-locked by concrete and suburban houses for a good fifty years or more, there's an amazing number of different tree species within the woods.

Since about the only thing I really know much about is trees, I was going through the woods one day with one of my twin daughters and I was showing off by identifying all the different trees for her and giving her both the common name and the Latin names for the trees. Pretty impressive you say. Yeah, I was impressed too; that I even remembered all of them. But I had gotten to about twenty-five different trees, and I had gotten all of the Latin names right and my daughter was so impressed with how smart I was, and I was so impressed with how smart I was to remember all those names, especially the Latin. And as I was patting myself on the back for being so brilliant, it struck me how vain I could be, and just how vain people can be in general. I realized how much we seemed to need to pet our own egos on a pretty regular basis. I mean, just a little thing like having a good memory and I was strutting about like a peacock for being so smart and brilliant.

Here's the thing. There's something about the human condition that just naturally makes us want to exalt ourselves at every opportunity. We simply have to show off and make ourselves look great. Why is that? Why do our egos need such feeding? Why do they need such constant stroking? I don't know the answer to that question and I pose it more or less rhetorically, but with Christmas right around the corner I think it's a pretty good thing to ponder a little.

I just had a 50th birthday party this past year and it was a great celebration with all my friends and family. I was just the center of all attention. Yet we're about to celebrate Christmas, which started as a holiday to celebrate the single most important birth in all of mankind, a birth that essentially went pretty much un-noticed as it happened; and gathered around this momentous birth were maybe a few shepherds, and maybe a couple of ox and lambs - not particularly royal digs. In fact, you could say it was a birth in the most humble, least exalted conditions you could imagine for the most important figure born into man-kind.

Now the celebration of this birth has turned into something quite different these days, and the real reason we started celebrating has all but been forgotten for a lot of us. I don't want to ruin anybody's Christmas, but the reason for the celebration has been twisted, and turned and forgotten over the years. I think what's happened is the same thing that happened to me in the woods as I patted myself on the back for remembering my Latin tree names. It's just the natural human condition to minimize God and exalt ourselves at almost every opportunity. For the very least thing we will heap mountains of praise upon ourselves. For doing things only a decent god-fearing person SHOULD do, we endlessly pat ourselves on the back and give ourselves praise. For making one moral choice, which shouldn't have even been a choice at all, we elevate ourselves to saints and angels, riding the first class section on the express train to heaven. Yes, we're all very good at elevating ourselves in our own hearts and minds. But I think we risk a lot by doing so.

I hope you never feel I'm lecturing during the "Loon Moment". If anything, I'm lecturing myself, and you just happen to be around to receive the fall-out.

The child that rose from those humble beginnings in a manager several thousand years ago lived a life as humble as the lowest among us today. Then He died for us without ever uttering a complaint. Throughout his life He only told us we had to do one thing.

And what He said, and what He told us to do was this – *"I, if I be lifted up from the earth, I will draw all men unto Me"*. And He further said *"The words that I speak unto you, they are spirit and they are life"*......

The really tough part about believing in Christmas as the birth of Jesus Christ, incidentally our Lord and Savior, as opposed to the atheist secularists, who believe we're just carrying on a pagan tradition of celebrating the winter solstice is this: as soon as you're feeling like a genius for having remembered all your Latin names while on a nice stroll in the woods, or as soon as you're done patting yourself on the back for <u>once</u> doing the right thing out of the hundreds of times you're given an opportunity, and when you're all done pointing to yourself as the best example of a human being God ever created, you get reminded of an event so special and of someone so unique, who took human form on a Christmas day over 2000 years ago. In the most humble of surroundings and with no fanfare, the only perfect human who ever walked this earth was born. He told us to lift Him up before all mankind. We don't seem do it so often throughout the year, so maybe, just maybe, we can do it for a few moments on His birthday. Give it a try this Christmas. And that is the "Loon Moment" for today.

From the "Loon Moment"- Dec. 23, 2006

Here's what I added a few years later:

When I first began to revise "Loon Moments", I took the liberty of rearranging the order of the broadcasts and stories. There wasn't any real need or any particular purpose in changing their sequence, and I'm not sure what possessed me to it; I just did it. As it turns out, this broadcast ended up last, and now that it is, I'm glad it turned out this way. It gives me an opportunity to end this book and leave you with a special and important message.

Writing and publishing this book has been something I really needed to do. I've heard it said, a lot of authors can't go on to write anything else until they complete their autobiography. I guess the cathartic nature of writing such a work, and spilling your life out for the world to see, is somehow supposed to free you up and allow you to move on to bigger and better things. For me, "Loon Moments" is the closest thing I'll ever get to an autobiography. I've got way too much dirty laundry in my hamper to ever write a "tell all" autobiography. Hell, I'm trying to forget chapters in my life and do better, not relive them. So "Loon Moments" is a close as I'll come and it's good enough for me. And yet, it's been a cleansing experience all the same. Because in most of these stories, there is something which made me reflect on an important value or principle. And as I re-read the broadcast above, I knew there was a final one I wanted to leave with all of you.

There's only been one perfect human being to walk this planet, and none of us can ever reach that level of perfection here on earth. But for all our human failings, and for all our weaknesses, we never have to be ashamed of ourselves if only we continue to try to be like Him. I don't mean pay lip service to, I mean truly try. It's a little contradictory to the common "self-help" wisdom of our day. They're always telling us to set reasonable goals, those we can reach and achieve. In so doing, the idea is to build on our successes. But unfortunately, that flies in the face of the human being 'operating manual' as written by the man himself. It's completely 180 degrees off center. He tells us our goal should be something we know is unattainable; to be like Christ.

I don't know about you, but in a way I think it's pretty nice to have an unattainable goal. There nothing like certain and pre-ordained failure to really take the pressure off. Fortunately, I think we're all going to be judged by how hard we try, not whether or not we are able to fully succeed. If we've all got to be perfect and 100% Christ-like in order to get into heaven, then hell is going to be one crowded place.

Now I hate to end up on a political note, but I can't help myself and it really does emphasize the point I'm trying to make. You see, liberals don't see any value in striving for the unattainable. For them, it's easier to take an atheist, humanist point of view. If we just tell ourselves all of our bad behavior is part of the human condition, unavoidable, or better yet, natural and something we should celebrate, then we have free license to continue. Seems risky to me, but what do I know?

Conservatives on the other hand, recognize bad behavior for what it is, they repent and strive to do better next time. For this we're generally ridiculed and called hypocrites. I think I'm going to keep on trying even if I'm considered a striving, failing, hypocrite. It seems a little safer. I don't know about you, but I think throwing in the towel altogether and using that psycho-babble for justification is more risk than I'm willing to take.

So keep trying and don't be too hard on yourself when you fail. You're going to, that's for sure. Just truly resolve and honestly try to do better next time and know perfection is unattainable in this life. Take a moment to treasure and be truly thankful for the "Loon Moments" God gives us all to enjoy; gifts of family, friends and the wonderful, awe-inspiring beauty which is nature. And that is the "Loon Moment" for today.

Scott Franz – February 2009

www.ingramcontent.com/pod-product-compliance
Lightning Source LLC
LaVergne TN
LVHW011401080426
835511LV00005B/381